Blue Water Men — And Women

Blue Water Men – And Women

by

FRED HUMISTON

PORTLAND, MAINE

GUY GANNETT PUBLISHING CO.

Dedicated to the great seafarers of Maine, and their descendants whose response to the Press Herald daily column, "Blue Water Men — And Women" has done so much to encourage the the author and spur publication of this book.

INTRODUCTION

Newspapers have perhaps become better known for publishing in serial form that which has appeared in book. This volume is a reversal of that situation. "Blue Water Men – And Women" has already substantially appeared in the Portland Press Herald where it proved an immensely popular feature for the nine months over which the articles extended.

It is in response to an unprecedented demand by Press Herald readers, and others who have heard of the series, that the collection of columns has been re-edited for this more permanent record.

The book is the work of newspaper columnist and historian Fred Humiston and deals with the seafarers of Maine in their greatest period, the nineteenth century.

E. F.

CONTENTS

FOREWORD

THE TREND TOWARD informality in modern historical writing offers an especially appropriate format for this story of the Blue Water folk; Yankees who were informal to a degree, yet had a severe sense of dignity. It is in an effort to recreate the atmosphere of those brave times, and the temper of the men and women who changed the course of history even as they made it, that the author has so freely used the vernacular.

Few of the events narrated in this book are more than one hundred and fifty years old. Some happened as recently as sixty years ago, so it is evident that in Maine the past is never far away, and reminders of it are everywhere: the stately mansions of the shipmasters, the ancient meeting houses, the quaint villages, the crumbling wharves and ropewalks, even hulks of old ships lying lonely and wretchedly at the moorings, or heeled over on a mudflat, their bones beginning to show.

It is a proud heritage that can bring coastal Mainers to a pause in this jet age, to gaze wistfully toward an empty horizon.

Chapter One

A SPECIAL BREED OF MEN

FOR WELL OVER three centuries the sailing vessel dominated the Maine scene, directly influencing the economic, social and cultural structures, as well as furnishing an effective method of defense and attack.

Is it any wonder then that Mainers were said to have been born with salt water in their veins?

It was in the nineteenth century, however, that their exploits and prowess took on the mantle of legend with the advent of the Blue Water Men of Maine, who sailed tall ships of their own building on all the Seven Seas. These men were indeed a breed apart, and as long as a Mainer lives, or an American, so will their story. And in Maine especially, where the past and present go hand in hand, there are still oldsters with long memories who knew the tall ships, and to whom the past is but yesterday.

The Blue Water Men were not aware of being different. They considered themselves run-of-the-mill Mainers, with a job to do. And if the shipmasters held themselves aloof, it was only the accepted pattern of dignity worn as necessary to their profession.

Both youngsters and old men trod the quarterdeck, and both youngsters and old men served before the mast, and if they sailed deep water to distant lands, in fair weather and foul, they were entitled to that maritime distinction that knows no rank but worth.

To command and officer the great full-rigged ships demanded men of the highest caliber, with more than average ability in navigation and seamanship. It was assumed that their character and morals were of the same high standards, and as a rule this was so. It was always true in the early days, when all the crewmen were Yankees, and mostly neighbors, or neighbor boys. These were not hands to be "put upon." In such an event they would quickly show their resentment.

With the Fabulous Forties and the Roaring Fifties, and the sharp, high-bowed clipper to replace the old full-bodied ships, larger crews were required. Many Outlanders and even a few foreign foreigners were signed on. Naturally, where a mate might hesitate to be unduly severe with the lad from next door, he felt little compunction in telling off one from Massachusetts or York State.

With the Gold Rush to California, speed was king and passenger and freight rates so exorbitant that the owners paid bonuses to officers, and sometimes even to the crews, for record runs.

This was a situation that kept the entire ship's company keyed up, and the tension ran down the chain of command to the lowest level. It was the foremast hand who became the main target for officer irritation, and taken aback by such rude behavior he would remonstrate to the best of his ability.

But his ability in this respect, while remarkable, was completely overshadowed by the mate's, who made a point of acting on the time-honored military maxim that the best defense is offense. And it was from this humble beginning that the Bucko Mate evolved, a phenomenon which after the Civil War and the coming of the huge ships called Down Easters, reached the peak of perfection.

Just as the demand for speed directly brought into being the Bucko, so it turned many cautious captains into the wildest of Sail Carriers. The next logical step was to turn what had been a genial, even kindly master, into a ferocious Bully Captain.

Fortunately, while there were Sail Carriers aplenty, Bully Captains were few and far between.

Bucko Mates, on the other hand, were a dime a dozen, but only an ignoble few stood at the top of their profession. Mister Martin, Mister Ross, Mister Watts, Mister True and Mister Allen were among these. Mind, to be "up there" a Bucko had to be an expert seaman, know his ship, have ability in many lines, be the possessor of a mean disposition, a rugged physique and be the master of the manly arts. Aside from ready fists and stomping boots, his tools were belaying pins and knuckle dusters. And to give the Devil his due, it must be admitted that the Bucko Mate drove himself as hard as he drove the fore-mast hands.

Although the designation "Blue Water Man" was a distinction awarded any who experienced the pleasures and hardships of deep water voyaging over a period of years, a caste system did exist in the forecastle. The elite of these, the "Cape Horners," were the rugged men who had made the dangerous passage round the Horn, and the more he made the more elite he became. Captain Jim Murphy of Bath, for instance, was said to have made sixty such trips, believed to be the record.

"A Packet Rat" was a seaman who had not been round the Horn. He had plied his trade trans-Atlantic, from New York, Boston and Baltimore to Liverpool and other European ports. While a sailor of undoubted experience and ability he was, to the Horners, at the bottom of the maritime ladder; always excepting, of course, the "Flying Fish."

Both Cape Horners and Packet Rats sneered at the Flying Fish sailors, who got their title from a packet line of the same name running to the West Indies. Although these unruly gentlemen wouldn't admit it the scorn heaped on the Fish by the Horners and Rats was not for lack of seamanship but from envy.

The Flying Fish were super-de-luxe sailors, the rich men of the sea. Their wages were high and they were not dependent on the slop chest for their gear. They dressed well at all times and usually came aboard with several seabags, oilskins, extra seaboots and even a private "Donkey's Breakfast," the name given to a straw bed-tick. To add insult to injury they were often assisted by porters.

But if the Horners and Rats were scornful of the Fish, the latter looked down their aristocratic noses at the "ruffians" as the others were known to the Fish. A mate, Bucko or otherwise, however, was impartial. All he was interested in was how a foremast hand performed his duty, and he'd as soon blow down and stomp a Fish as he would a Rat.

One reason the so-called Packet Rats didn't take kindly to their title was that it was an especial designation for the "Blackballers," and Blackballers were very, very ugly customers.

They were proud of their name, which derived from the

fleet they served, the famous Black Ball Line, plying principally between New York and Liverpool. Its house flag was a black ball on a blue field, and every vessel in the fleet also had an oversized black ball painted on the bunt of her foretopsail. The Line was known, from its colors and for other obvious reasons, as the Black and Blue Line.

Its seamen were a hard bitten lot, from Liverpool mostly, with an earned reputation for being rum-soaked and ready-fisted. Always anxious to go as far as they could, many would jump ship at every port and carelessly sign on aboard another, often of the same line, to the pleased anticipation of mates who hadn't completed workovers on previous voyages.

Their customary manner in coming aboard was dead drunk; kicked if they could stagger, carried if too far gone. But when the rum was beaten out of them they were great seaman: with their other disadvantages they had to be.

The Horners and Blackballers were natural enemies, and shoreside, if the slur "Packet Rat" didn't start the fireworks, the Horners had another in reserve. This was "Baggage Smasher," a cry which was guaranteed to set a Blackballer almost to foaming at the mouth, with the resultant pleasure of a fine old free-for-all.

The Cape Horners as they grew older or became more experienced were given another name, a sort of coat-of-arms under the family crest. The term was "Shellback."

☆   ☆   ☆

Thus while it becomes apparent that all Blue Water Men were not Mainers, all Mainers who sailed the tall ships were Blue Water Men, and nearly all were Cape Horners with the heft of them Shellbacks.

Chapter Two

LONG EMBARGO SPELLS OPPORTUNITY

THE STORY OF the Blue Water Men properly begins with President Jefferson's "Long Embargo," which went into effect on December 22, 1807, as answer to the British and French raids on American shipping. For the next fourteen months no vessel could clear for a foreign port, and vessels in the coastwise trade were required to give bond that their cargoes would be landed only in United States ports.

At first the Maine merchants and shipmasters were in favor of the measure. General Abiel Wood of Wiscasset, and William King of Bath, representing the important financial groups for the District, hoped that it would bring the offending nations to a more reasonable attitude.

But spring passed, summer came, then the leaves began to fall, and still "reason" did not prevail. With the first snowfall it became apparent to even the dullest mind that the foreigners had no intention of mending their miserable ways. Meanwhile, American shippers were losing money and American seamen were out of work. The Embargo soon became unpopular.

Yankees had always been first-rate smugglers, from the Hancocks on down. Now some of the shipping people were inclined toward the opinion that it wouldn't be criminal to ignore a law that brought the grim specter of starvation to the doorstep of so many homes. Especially when it would only be occasionally; just often enough to make a modest profit that would keep the vessels in commission and body and soul together. Mainers had always made their living by way of the sea. Why should they stop because of a few lines penned on some foolscap?

To put this premise to test, fast craft were fitted out, usually topsail schooners, and crews of adventurous seamen signed on who would take the risk of getting them to open water. And when these initial efforts proved successful, others, previously timid, threw caution to the winds. Before you could

[5]

bend on a topsail, everybody and his uncle was ciphering on ways and means to send out the ventures of golden promise.

Never strangers to deep water, Mainers, through the colonial era and the years of the Revolution, had for economic reasons confined much of their shipping activity to the coastal and West India trade. Now those same reasons offered incentive for mass expansion.

The Americans were not alone in their Embargo-breaking. They were frequently — and gleefully — assisted in their undercover operations by Canadians in the Maritime Provinces, who were looked upon as Yankees under the skin.

American goods were smuggled to England through Canada, and to France through Spanish Florida. In the process everybody became happy, and rich, except the United States Government. But President Jefferson took a very dim view of this unpatriotic behavior and vowed to put a stop to it.

The logical region where the boom should be lowered was Maine, for Mainers were the worst offenders as well as the most efficient.

Added to the straight smuggling transactions, many an honest appearing coaster would clear a Maine port with cargoes allegedly for the American South. The vessel's log would then report the ship running into weather so ungodly foul that she was blown off her course — often clear across the Atlantic. In "dire distress" the Mainer would put into a European port for repair and refitting, then return across the ocean to deliver her cargo.

By some strange twist of fortune the cargo that had started from Maine as salt cod would reach its American destination as bulk salt, lemons, or something equally valuable. The Mainer then returned home with a regular southern cargo, warmed by the satisfaction of having outwitted the authorities and making triple profits from a single bonded coasting voyage.

A grim Mr. Jefferson, studying reports coming down from Maine, finally called a meeting of the Cabinet, inviting naval officers to sit in, among them the famous Captain Stephen Decatur of the U. S. Frigate *Chesapeake*.

☆   ☆   ☆

Almost overnight, Eastport had become the busiest of all the United States ports. Large flour consignments arrived daily from southern shipping points, and as many as fourteen of the carriers were anchored in the harbor at one time. One week brought thirty thousand barrels, and one hundred sixty thousand barrels were mysteriously disposed of in one year.

As the town had never hoped to carry on business enterprises of such magnitude, there were few warehouses and fewer wharves. Out of necessity, caches were made in likely spots along the shore, or on points where the heavy forests extended close to the Border.

The Federal agents were not asleep. Special deputies were sworn in. Sentries, well armed, were posted from West Quoddy to the Machias River, or other likely places — to no avail. Finally, guards were posted within twenty rods of each other all along the coast — but still the flour vanished!

With flour selling at four dollars a barrel in Eastport, and the value increasing three hundred percent by a two-mile voyage, Mainers were bound to find a way.

These conditions gave rise to a new industry — ferrying. Boats of every type were brought into use, from birch canoe to sturdy sloop. As the transportation risks increased, so did the freight rates. A pert worker often netted fifty dollars per night.

As the militia couldn't be trusted, a company of Regulars was sent to Eastport, followed by the frigate *Chesapeake*, Captain Decatur, trailed by four of the new *Jefferson* gunboats, to be on station in the rivers.

In 1808, Mainers who had been successful in circumventing Mr. Jefferson's Long Embargo became publicly reconciled to the measure. "In the face of Bulldog and Frog aggression," these grandiose smugglers blandly stated, "the Embargo is an actual necessity."

On the other hand there were Mainers who didn't profit by the circumstances. Many of this group were wealthy shipowners who soon wouldn't be if the Embargo persisted and their vessels rotted at the moorings.

Complaints were made to the authorities, who promptly employed additional agents, more informers and stepped up the coastal patrols. Key points such as Fort Popham at the mouth of the Kennebec were garrisoned with troops.

As time passed, the soldiers were pleased to discover that the local inhabitants were exceptionally cordial folk, and off-duty they accepted invitations to parties and informal gatherings as far upriver as Bath.

Finally, their hosts felt that the brave defenders of the Embargo had been softened up sufficiently for them to risk a trial run. "Nothing ventured, nothing gained," the Bath men sagely advised one another.

"But it's my vessel that'll take the risk," the owner protested. "Ever see the guns in that there fort?"

"Of course I have. Anyway, it's my cargo your vessel will be carrying," the backer replied.

"There's one thing you gentlemen seem to forget," the master of the vessel put in. "Should these fort gunners aim true, it'll be my head that'll be blown off."

The owner was shocked. "Merton, I never suspected you of being a coward. If I didn't know better I'd say you were an Outlander."

As a result of this interesting conversation the ship *Sally* dropped down the Kennebec one wintry February night in 1809. It was the dark of the moon, the sky was covered with scud clouds and a spit of snow occasionally struck the anxious faces of those aboard. Occasionally too a star or several stars would gleam briefly, dimly, yet enough to silhouette a moving bulk against the water.

Coming abreast of Fort Popham the *Sally's* company held its collective breath.

Suddenly every gun in the fort seemed to go off together; surely the clap of doom for the daring little smuggler.

But evidently the entertainment of the past had paid off for the friendly gunners aimed high, merely cutting some of the rigging and putting one roundshot through the topsail. The tide was on the ebb and soon *Sally* was past the Sugar Loaves, Pond Island and Seguin, and a course was set for the British Isles.

Her cargo of lumber was sold in London for an immense sum, one that laid the foundation for the fortune of a famous Bath shipbuilding family. Which proves that taking a risk is often warranted.

Nonetheless, the venture was not repeated, for it resulted in one of Mr. Jefferson's terrier-like gunboats being stationed off Parker's Flats.

That, then, was one aspect of the *Sally's* voyage to fame and fortune, but there was another, more amusing, that stemmed from the character of her company.

They were all Kennebec Mainers, and Kennebeckers were always almighty suspicious of one another in money matters, although ready to band together against outsiders. When the fort with its garrison of Regulars was passed, that need was over and they were free to resume the *status quo*.

At the bottom of the trouble were two sea lawyers, the cook and the bosun, both good men from a professional standpoint but more than ready to stand up for their rights and those of their fellow crewmen.

"You fellers know what the owners are up to," one or other of this worthy pair would say whenever he had the opportunity. "We've got a fortune in lumber aboard, yet who gets the profits? The owners, by Jupiter! And whose hides are being risked? Our'n. It ain't right an' I say let's do something about it."

"You mean mutiny?" a foremast hand asked, aghast.

"This ship ain't got no papers, inasmuch as she sailed secretly and agin the law, so it can't be no mutiny," the sea lawyer would reply.

Finally, at a secret meeting the crew determined to protect and enforce its believed rights. Accordingly, in a well-planned and efficiently executed *coup*, the officers were made prisoner and locked up separately.

Now all that the crew needed do was hold to the course as set, until terms could be reached.

A committee next informed each officer that to be liberated it was only necessary to sign a pledge that each crew member would receive a bonus of fifty dollars when the cargo was sold in London. Grudgingly, the master, the mate and the super-cargo agreed.

The crew was overjoyed, and to show there was no hard feeling on their part worked with a will to make amends for the short lapse in discipline. And, as the officers seemed to show no ill feeling, all were happy as the ship sailed toward the golden haze of the future.

The crew, however, shrewd Mainers though they were, forgot or overlooked the fact that their officers were even more calculating.

When the supercargo came down with a sudden sickness they were deeply concerned, for he was after all a neighbor boy. Putting in close to Land's End they manned a boat to row him ashore for medical attention and left him there with little hopes that he would live to see his native Kennebec again.

But hardly had they settled down to rowing back to the anchored *Sally* than the "poor boy" was ahorse and whipping his way furiously on the road to London Town.

When the embargo-dodger docked, the supercargo was waiting with a throng of Crown officials, everybody, it seemed, from Bow Street Runners up to the Prime Minister.

The entire crew was arrested on the frightening charge of mutiny, then visited in their dungeon by the treacherous supercargo and the *Sally's* smug master. "All we need do is sign the complaints and press the charges, and you boys will be old men before you see Maine again — if you don't hang. On the other hand, return the written promises that we signed under duress, and the charges will be dropped, at our request."

The crew sadly returned the agreements. On the return voyage they were comforted by the consoling knowledge that they had almost outsmarted the officers. "If only they hadn't been same as us — Mainers!"

☆   ☆   ☆

And so ended the Saga of the *Sally*, or the heft of it, but the smuggling operations continued, and from *Sally's* example took on a deep-sea flavor, Maine ships bearing Maine products to markets in distant lands. The risk was greater and the initial investment requirements larger, but the profits were in keeping.

In the Kennebec area, the master minds of unlawful venture were usually in Bath, but the action department was generally recruited downriver. The old store at Phippsburg Center was the Headquarters for the smugglers; a sort of clearing house for both big and small outfits. The proprietors, Hill and Cobb, were as "Honest as the day was long." (The days were shorter in winter.) Anyway, smuggling was not considered truly criminal; never had been. And the best people were involved.

It was on the Phippsburg store scales that the gold pieces brought back by the *Adoniram* were weighed, after her successful voyage to Demarara. The *Adoniram* had stood on and off south of Monhegan as cargoes from towns all along the coast were loaded aboard from whaleboats, thereby outsmarting the the Government agents who were watching for her close to shore. When she returned, it was to Phippsburg for division of the profits.

What had started out in Maine as small ventures "just to keep vessels in commission and body and soul together," had got out of hand to such an extent that some of the smuggling operations took on the pattern of modern gangster activity.

For example, on one moonless night, close to forty friends of Hill and Cobb gathered in the brick store, local men with shares in the current venture. The *Mary Jane*, lying at the end of the wharf ready to go, was armed with cannon primed to defy the Custom House boat or even the big guns of the fort at Popham.

Although the brig was fast and it was hoped could clear the river's mouth without a battle, she carried in addition to her regular crew, thirty men to work the guns and resist boarders. Among these were twelve that today would be designated "goons." They were under special contract to get the vessel clear, come what may. None weighed less than two hundred pounds and all were hardened fighters. Each was disguised in the manner of a commando, with soot-blackened face.

When Kennebec men made an investment at this stage of their battle of wits with the authorities, they wanted it protected.

☆　☆　☆

For some Mainers the Long Embargo had spelled opportunity, but for the great majority it was a period of incredible hardship.

During the fourteen months that the Embargo was in force at least sixty per cent of the District's inhabitants were unem-

ployed. Soup kettles were set up in public squares, and even
some of the shipowners themselves were often forced to accept
dole to keep their families from starving.

Wiscasset, which had been a long-time leader in the lumber
trade, was especially hard hit. Just a year before the Embargo
the Custom House had issued sea letters to sixty-seven ships.
In 1808 only two were issued; nearly forty large vessels lay at
anchor along the river, together with smaller craft. They presented a sight to break the heart of any seafaring man as they
swung with the tide, sails unbent, spars sent down, Jefferson's
Nightcaps (inverted tar barrels) topping the lower masts.

When the Act of Embargo was repealed the day before
Jefferson retired from office the entire Atlantic seaboard celebrated, and New England especially went wild with delight.
Although the ban on trade with France and England was not
lifted for three months, President Madison, prematurely, issued
his proclamation in April.

The Yankees had blamed Jefferson for their troubles: first
because he was a Southerner; second because the Embargo was
his idea. They had even written a song about it, and him.

> "Our ships all in motion once whitened the ocean
> They sailed and returned with a cargo,
> Now doomed to decay, they have fallen prey
> To Jefferson, worms and Embargo."

Well, they had gotten rid of Jefferson and his Embargo
at one and the same time. Of course, Mr. Madison was a Vir-
ginian, too, but he seemed fairly decent in spite of it.

Amid the general rejoicing, the staid, sour-faced Yankees,
as personified by the Mainers, broke loose from their moorings.
At Wiscasset the celebration was better than the Fourth of
July, and far noisier. Captain John Binney, commander of
the Fort, describes the events.

"At the request of Mayor Wood I fired from the Battery
abreast of the town four 24-pounders, and the citizens from
their subscription kept firing until ten at night. At 7 a procession was formed headed by the aforesaid companies . . . and all
the citizens of the town followed 4 deep about 250 men, 500 boys,
700 dogs observed by 800 women, 900 children and 1000 cats
besides other animals in great number. The procession went

through the streets and at convenient distances gave three cheers . . . drums beating, fifes playing, Bells a-ringing, marshals hallooing, guns firing, altogether made the most noisome hurlebello you ever heard.

"After parading through the town the whole company went to Fort Hill where grog in pails was given to the common people and they were bid to get roaring drunk as soon as possible. The Gentlemen went to Dows where Brandy rum & wine were in abundance; they drank Madison's health, the cups went merrily round and songs were sung . . ."

Captain Binney's account was not a complete one, not by a jug full, but there were few next morning who could have recounted more. It had really been quite unnecessary to bid a mob of celebrating Mainers to "get roaring drunk as soon as possible."

Chapter Three

"THERE'S MONEY IN IT"

THE EMBARGO ENDED, every port was a scene of extraordinary
activity. Vessels were being repaired and refitted, mounting
piles of cargoes crowded the wharves, everybody was planning
to make money, and some already were.

Asa Clapp of Portland fitted out his *North America* for the
Russian trade. She sailed with a mixed cargo; one apt to appeal
to the people of that northern land. The principal items on the
manifest were logwood and mahogany, coffee, pepper, indigo,
and that famous New England product, rum. Her return cargo
consisted of iron, hemp, sheeting, duck, sailcloth and bristles.
The profits from this single venture were enormous.

Clapp and his partner, Matthew Cobb, also owned a little
brig, the *Lee*, which they sent out. The venture netted them
eighty thousand dollars.

This prosperity was too good to last. Although Mr. Madison continued his efforts toward peace and reaching satisfactory
agreements with the belligerent nations, a group of young men
in Congress were a stumbling block. Known as "War Hawks,"
they were just that, and powerful enough to bring pressure to
bear on the President.

In April of 1812, a ninety-day embargo was laid. This was
to allow American vessels to return safely to home ports. As
might be expected, the reverse took place. Those already in
port headed for the open sea.

On June 18, 1812, Congress declared war on Great Britain,
five days after her government had revoked its Orders in Coun-
cil, the principal excuse for the American declaration.

The news of Parliament's peaceful gesture came too late,
brought by a Wiscasset ship which arrived on August 6th.

The War was immediately unpopular in New England.
"Free Trade and Sailor's Rights" was the battle cry of the War
Hawks, representatives of farmers and tradesmen of the West
and South who had never seen a ship.

In the northeast, mass meetings were held in protest: 246 voters in Wells, Maine, stood for peace; only four voted for war. A memorial was then sent to the President of the United States, declaring the war to be "unjust, unnecessary and inexpedient." At Bath, a convention of Lincoln County voters condemned the Government in no uncertain terms.

Hardly had Mr. Madison and his Secretary of State read the many and varied memorials from Maine, when a Maine vessel, quite by "accident," captured a British vessel. Both were officially unarmed. The cargo was worth a considerable sum, and when it and the enemy craft were condemned and sold in a prize court, the surprised Mainers netted a handsome profit.

From that time on, Mainers didn't speak out so forcefully against Mr. Madison's War. Instead, they spent a deal of time quietly ciphering, then moved down to the shipyards and started work on such craft as could only be used as "letters-of-marque and reprisal."

☆ ☆ ☆

When the Mainers, with the other New Englanders, discovered that huge sums of money could be made in privateering, every shipyard was busy and men were standing in line to sign on aboard vessels already commissioned.

Nor was money the whole of it. Patriotism entered the picture, somewhat belatedly, it is true, but it was there. Seafaring, though, is a rough and dangerous calling, even in times of peace. In war, there was the constant danger of being sunk, taken prisoner or killed. So if a man could combine business and patriotism, wasn't that his privilege?

Topsail schooners and brigs were the favorite craft among the Maine privateersmen. Fast, they were able to carry sizeable crews for boarding and to sail prizes back home. They could also carry sufficient iron to fight off a Bulldog of the same class, or larger if cornered. As a matter of sound business, such engagements were to be avoided, if possible.

Enemy merchantmen were to be taken almost anywhere, and were, but it was the Mainers who discovered the weak point in mighty England's armor.

This weak point was the narrow seas that give access to her main ports. The Yankees, like John Paul Jones before them, now sailed to the Big Opportunity. Based in the French

Channel ports, they took a frightening toll of British shipping, and Lloyd's Bell rang out the sad news to the underwriters so regularly, that they learned to live with its doleful clang. Yet it did not mean that they accepted the situation.

The alarm of British business was reflected by the London Times for February 11, 1815.

"The American cruisers daily enter among our convoys, seize prizes in sight of those that should afford protection, and if pursued, 'put on their sea wings.' . . . It must be encouraging to Mr. Madison to read the logs of his cruisers. If they fight, they are sure to conquer; if they fly, they are sure to escape."

The privateer fleet from Casco Bay alone consisted of forty-five vessels, as officially listed. They ranged in size from the tiny four-ton *Lark*, with a crew of four men, her only armament four muskets, to the great *Hyder Ally* of 367 tons, a crew of one hundred men, and sixteen sizeable guns.

Nearly all the Maine privateers were successful, the few exceptions usually a matter of bad luck. The privateer schooner *Gleaner* of Wells offers a sad example.

The unfortunate *Gleaner* was one of the first hastily-built vessels; a community venture of the people of Wells, who were enthusiastic over the project. Completely outfitted and carrying six guns and a crew of fifty eager-beavers, she was sent to make their fortunes.

The cruise started favorably enough. Right at the outset the *Gleaner* sighted a likely prize, gave chase, overhauled and took her. A prize crew was put aboard and she was sent into port. Almost immediately the *Gleaner* spied another victim, but while she was making her second capture a British sloop-of-war likewise swooped down. The *Gleaner* and her would-be second prize were taken to Halifax. In Wells the bottom dropped out of the privateer market.

The Casco Bay privateer fleet's pride and joy, the huge *Hyder Ally*, had, curiously enough, been designed as a merchantman. Launched from the yard of Samuel Fickett, at the foot of Park Street, Portland, her keel had been laid long before war was declared or even considered.

Even so she had been so constructed to carry a battery, for roving pirates posed a constant peacetime threat. Her builder

Fickett's motto was: "If you carry guns at all, carry enough to be effective."

As her hull took form and grew, observers noted that her lines were sharper than those of a merchant vessel need be, and presumed she had been designed for smuggling. But when she was finally launched and christened, registered for three hundred sixty-seven tons, it soon became evident that Fickett had built her to sell.

Fickett had chosen a bad time and eventually closed a deal with the Boston firm of Bryant and Sturgis who paid him forty dollars per ton, his asking price, only on condition that he would rig what he had intended as a brig, into a ship.

It was shortly after he had this task under way that the United States declared war on Great Britain. With the unprecedented demand which followed for anything that would sail, Fickett could have received eighty dollars per ton without the trouble and expense of re-rigging.

Where poor Fickett had been unlucky, the Boston firm of Bryant and Sturgis were not only pleased with their purchase of a fine new ship at fifty percent below current war prices, they ran into more good luck.

They intended to use the *Hyder Ally* as a privateer, but they would need to arm her and guns were at a premium. Then they were informed that the guns of the captured war brig *Boxer* had been sold at auction by the Government and could be obtained through a private sale. These were purchased for a song, and adding some new pieces, the ship was armed. Twelve eighteen pound carronades, two long eighteen pounders, and two long nines for bow and stern chasers. Official naval craft of the privateer's class were seldom commissioned with better armament.

Israel Thorndike of Beverly was her captain, the first officer Henry Oxnard of Portland. The second was one Perry of Salem, the third Noah Edgecomb of Portland. At this time she carried a crew of fifty men, nearly all Portlanders.

The *Hyder Ally* cleared Portland Harbor in January, 1814, and set a course for the Indian Ocean, said to be a promising hunting ground filled with fat East Indiamen.

It was too, the only trouble being that the British East India Company maintained its own navy, backed up by the Royal Navy. And sure enough, off the Cape of Good Hope, the Portland privateer was sighted by a sloop-of-war belonging to the Company. The Bulldog promptly changed course and bore down, the bone in his teeth.

Captain Thorndike was half-minded to come about and give battle. The alarmed Henry Canard didn't dare ask, "Are ye tetched?" but looked as if he would like to. Instead, the mate pointed out that a sloop-of-war of that class would carry at the very least, twenty-eight guns and one hundred fifty men.

"What of it?"

"We have only sixteen guns and fifty men."

"Mister Oxnard," the Captain said severely. "You are forgetting what evens the odds."

"Sir?"

"We are Americans; most of us Mainers. However, regardless of my own inclinations, my first duty is to the owners. It is to their interest that we go away from here — fast."

The First and everybody aboard heaved a deep sigh of relief, as the *Hyder Ally,* putting on canvas, showed the enemy a clean pair of heels.

The flight paid off, for a short time later the privateer captured a real fat Indiaman, fairly bulging with valuable cargo. A prize crew was put aboard and she was ordered in to Portland. Although all Mainers, they were a trifle dubious over their own chances, considering the thousands of miles of ocean to be covered, swarming with enemy craft.

Off the coast of Sumatra the ship took two more prizes; English merchantmen with cargoes of pepper in bulk. Crews were put aboard and the huge vessels were sailed Maineward. This left the *Hyder Ally* short-handed, her first and second officers also gone with the prizes.

Captain Thorndike now adopted the ancient practice of privateers and pirates; that of using a different ensign for every occasion. So the Mainer was flying the Union Jack when she overhauled two Chinese junks, laden with betel nuts, silks and other goods of great value.

Naturally, the misguided Chinese protested that they were neutrals, not subject to seizure. Thorndike, with that keen sense of justice that earmarked the Yankee privateersman, condemned the cargoes as British property. "Leastwise," he explained to the distraught owners, "If they weren't now, they were liable to be, some time or another." So by taking the cargoes now, he, Thorndike, saved everybody trouble.

The immense wealth was shifted to the hold of the *Hyder Ally,* and the crestfallen Chinese were given ballast in return.

The captain knew that he would need all his Yankee sharpness to continue the voyage and bring it to a satisfactory conclusion. If he met a Bulldog, he would not dare fight it, even one of the privateer's class; he had hardly enough men to work the ship, let alone the guns. And for all her sharp lines and fast-sailing, it took men aplenty to work a full-rigged ship.

Too successful, overloaded and short-handed, the Mainers wondered what really would happen should they run into a Bulldog. They soon found out.

Sighted by the British frigate *Salsetta,* the privateer ran for it, the Bulldog in hot pursuit. Then to the company's horrified concern, the wind fell off and both vessels lay becalmed for twelve hours. It was now that the British had the advantage, for they lowered boats that took the frigate in tow. As they had more boats and men to row them, they were slowly creeping closer. Once within shooting range. . .

Then the wind sprang up. In the long chase that followed, the frigate banged away with the bowchasers, without effect. Its captain crowded on all canvas, yet could not quite close for the kill. Even low in the water the *Hyder Ally* was a slightly faster sailer.

Yet Captain Thorndike was not satisfied, and setting his mind to the problem he came up with an answer revolutionary in that era.

He set Chips and his mates to knocking out the woodwork from the stern of the ship, then worked two of the Long Toms down close enough to depress the muzzles of the big guns. He then rigged long breechings to hold the recoil, muttered a quick prayer and ordered them to be fired.

The discharge, entering the water close astern, helped propel the privateer even further from the pursuing frigate until, taking advantage of a sudden squall, she was able to make good her escape.

This was the first time the principles of jet propulsion were used to increase the speed of a ship. A Yankee captain figured it out, using double powder for fuel. The year was 1814.

☆   ☆   ☆

The Patriots had taken a dim view of the mass migration of the American Tories to Nova Scotia and New Brunswick (at that time one large province) during the Revolution. Now, in the War of 1812, they were glad the runouts had prospered for it put money in their pockets.

Halifax was the main enemy port for the Province, and the sea lanes leading from the Old Country to Halifax and up the St. Lawrence were rich hunting grounds for the swarming privateers.

The Mainers were especially delighted. Here was a new source of income; the best they had ever had. During the War, eighty-nine prize vessels were sent into Maine ports, and the United States Marshal for the District was a busy man indeed.

In August of the first year, the converted New York pilot boat *Teazer* sent four captures into Portland. Two had a combined value of two hundred thirty thousand dollars.

The Portsmouth privateer *Thomas* escorted a brig and a ship into Wiscasset. The ship was worth three hundred fifty thousand dollars. This was big money, and it was hoped the War would continue for some time.

The local people had it made. Not only did they take prizes on their own account, but the Outland captures were sent to Maine ports to be condemned and sold because it was safer.

The privateer ship *America,* most successful of the Bay State hunters, sent a fat prize into Bath. The cargo of silk was so valuable that the owners paid ten thousand dollars to have it sent overland to Boston.

The privateer *Viper* of New York sent the full-rigged ship *Victory* and two smaller vessels into Camden, where they were sold.

What remains a mystery to historians is why the Royal Navy let the Yankees get away with it. True, that Navy had its hands full with the new American frigates, but not in the first year of the War. Whatever the reason, Americans made the most of it, and reaped a golden sea harvest that started many fortunes.

One of the most famous Maine privateers, and one of the first to be built and launched (in five weeks, soon after war was declared), was the *Dart* of South Portland.

The *Dart* took a number of prizes, but it was her fifth that made her name famous in maritime history. This was when she sighted and gave chase to the brig *Dianna*, out of London, bound for Quebec.

This fame did not come from the rig, quality or size of the vessel taken, but from her cargo; 212 puncheons of rum. All rum was heavenly nectar to Yankees, but this was a special rum, having matured in the casks for many years in vaults on the London docks.

The captain and mate of the *Dart* took small samples of the cargo, and at the beatific expressions on their faces, the watching crewmen crowded closer. The captain wasn't mean, but he didn't dare let the men taste what was in those casks; not if he wanted to get back to Portland. So a day and night guard was put over the cargo, and it did arrive safely in port.

For years, the mere mention of "old *Dart* rum from the original casks" brought excited gleams to the eyes of connoisseurs everywhere, and as long as it lasted the fortunate Portlanders with a supply in their cellars were seldom without house guests.

As for the *Dart*, she sailed the seas constantly in search of a duplicate prize, and never found one. She cruised and cruised, until finally she didn't return. Her design was blamed for it, for she had a sharp pinque-like stern, and it was thought she had been overtaken by a following sea.

That's what the marine experts said, but the more superstitious hold that the *Dart* is still cruising the misty seas of eternity, determined to take another prize with a cargo of heavenly rum.

☆   ☆   ☆

One of the most successful Maine privateers was the Freeport-built *Dash*. Launched in 1813 from the Brewer yard at Porter's Landing on the Harraseeket River, for her Portland owners, merchants Seward and Samuel Porter, she was a "lucky" vessel from the start of her sea-going career.

Of 222 tons burthen, and pierced for sixteen guns, she was rigged as a topsail schooner. Fast and sleek, she seemed to fairly fly over the water, yet her people weren't satisfied. They knew she could do better. "Way she's built, she can carry a lot more canvas," her master said. "Under different rig, of course."

The rig of the *Dash* was changed from that of a topsail schooner to that of a hermaphrodite brig — square-rigged forward and schooner-rigged aft. Added to this, she carried a ringtail; a light sail bent on a long sliding spar and fitted to the main boom. Hoisted to the gaff as needed, it increased the spread of her mainsail by one-third.

Once she was carrying all canvas, the chase could never escape the *Dash*, nor, if the positions were reversed, could the privateer be overhauled. A sweet-sailing craft, it was popularly claimed she "never suffered defeat, never attacked an enemy's ship in vain, was never injured by hostile shot and knew no equal in speed."

She made seven cruises, under four masters. In the order named, they were Edward Kelleran, William Cammett, George Bacon and John Porter. She took and sent in fifteen prizes. Everyone made port safely and sold at a substantial profit. Yes, it was truly said that the *Dash* was lucky; that she bore a charmed life — or so it seemed.

Portlanders were mighty proud of their lucky privateer, and when in port she was the center of attention, with a stream of visitors. When she sailed, the wharves and harbor shipping were crowded, ensigns dipped and cheers went up.

It was so on her last voyage. She headed out with her usual snap and vim, the cheers behind her, her people proud and eager, with no inkling at all that Fate had decided that the luck of the *Dash* was ended.

She cleared the harbor in company with the *Champlain*, a new privateer. Captain Porter, twenty-four, was in command. He had said fond farewell to his bride of a few months, and looked forward to more adventure, and incidentally, profit.

The *Champlain* was out-classed; the *Dash*, at the end of the first day, had her hull-down. The wind freshened with the coming of night and a sudden squall hit them. Aboard the *Champlain* they saw the light of the *Dash* disappear in the scud. As the water was rapidly shoaling, the new privateer altered her course.

The *Dash* was never seen again. It was generally believed she foundered off George's Bank. She went down with her young captain, his two brothers, the mates and sixty able seamen.

Her loss was a great blow to Maine, but some people were extremely happy when they heard the sad news: Lloyd's of London, and the British naval command at Halifax. The *Dash* had been a nagging thorn in their sides.

Chapter Four

PIRATES AND THE WEST INDIA TRADE

MAINE MARINERS have always used vessels and rigs adaptable to their current trades, whether it be war or peace, so during Mr. Madison's War, when small, fast-sailing craft were required for the hit-and-run tactics of the privateers, they already had vessels of the desired rigs; topsail schooners and brigs. Easy to handle, they were able to sail circles round an enemy merchantman, or show a Bulldog a clean pair of heels, yet they were large enough to carry sufficient iron to fight when necessary, as well as being roomy enough for extra hands for boarding and prize crews.

With the Treaty of Ghent, the Mainers found these vessels to be particularly adapted to the "Old West India Trade." Large as needed for cargo space, with armament and war-experienced crews to fight off the hordes of pirates that infested those dangerous and poorly charted waters, the tops'l schooners and brigs were just the ticket.

So from the end of the War until 1840, Yankee rigs of this type were found everywhere in Spanish waters, and the Dons didn't take kindly to it, for the Islanders would rather trade with Maine than Spain or the Spanish possessions. But the Spaniards couldn't do much about it, except give the pirates their blessing, and material encouragement, as they preyed openly on American commerce.

The vessels used by the Mainers averaged about two hundred tons, although from 1830 on vessels of three hundred tons or larger were built. This was when the small full-rigged ships were beginning to come into use. Like the brigs, they were of a rather shallow draft, able to work their way into the numerous small rivers or creeks on which the island plantations were located.

These little ships were full-bodied in design and could, therefore, load more cargo than a brig or tops'l schooner, but as proponents of the last two rigs pointed out, what was the advantage of increasing cargo space at the expense of speed, thereby running the risk of capture?

It was an argument that never ended, and it was the favorite topic of maritime debate from Eastport to Havana.

Although the brig has been obsolete for nearly a hundred years, the period of the Old West India Trade was one where it was pre-eminent.

The brig was peculiarly American, with Maine having close to a monopoly on its construction. Mainers had always favored them, even over the topsail schooners, and it was common knowledge that the schooners were as fast a rig as ever has been contrived.

There was something special about a brig; a sort of Yankee independence, a forthrightness that was the very personification of the Yankee spirit. All the romance of the sea seemed to be in her sharp-prowed hull, usually painted black with a yellow streak, and in the raked masts and canvas smartly set under the Stars and Stripes. And if, when need be, the ports were triced up, the muzzles of her carronades watched the possible offender like so many unblinking eyes; stern reminders that these vessels were not to be easily trifled with.

Maine's full-rigged brig had both masts raked, in three spars. Main and fore were wholly square-rigged, except that on the mainmast was a standing gaff to which was bent a small fore-and-aft sail known as a spanker.

The snow, another Maine favorite, and probably in use before the brig, had much the same rig, the difference being that the snow set her spanker on a trysail mast that was stepped on deck a foot or so abaft the mainmast and secured aloft to its trestle-trees.

The Mainers were constantly experimenting with design and rig, so it was only a matter of time before the hermaphrodite brig was developed from the brig and snow. A cross between a brig and a schooner, she was square-rigged on the foremast and fore-and-aft rigged on the mainmast.

Once this new rig was proved, it was favored by the always expense-minded Yankees for her economy in men and gear.
Fewer hands were needed to work her, she was fast, and soon
became popular.

Most people, the English, for example, would have been
satisfied with this rig, and inclined to let-well-enough-alone.
Not the experimenting Mainers. If square sails work on the
foremast, why not on the mainmast? "But Godfrey," objectors
were quick to point out, "that's just the way the brig was rigged.
You'll be right back where you started from."

The experimenters naturally gave no heed to such careless
conversation and went right ahead with their experimenting to
evolve the "jackass brig," a vessel that carried one or more
square sails on the mainmast.

In Outlander waters this rig was called a brigantine. This,
of course, was totally incorrect. On the Maine coast, a brigantine carried the rig of a brig on her foremast, but the rig of
a tops'l schooner on her mainmast. That is, two spars for
square sails and a big fore-and-aft main as a powerful pusher
when close-hauled to the wind.

"What about cargo space?" the critics asked.

"Same as the tops'l schooner, she's faster and can do with
less. She gets her cargo to destination before slower craft,
bringing better prices."

In the heat of the century-old controversy, the once extremely popular tops'l sloop has practically been forgotten. In
fact, few people ever heard of the rig. In his "Hardscrabble,"
Elijah Kellogg gives a vivid description of a tops'l sloop.

"In addition to her mainsail, she carried a full suit of
square sails; course, topsail, top gallant sail and royal. Her
lower mast was rather short in proportion to the top, top-gal-
lant and royal masts. The mainmast was set well aft, and raked
a good deal. The bowsprit and jib-boom were long. She had a
sprit-sail yard and double martingale. The forebraces led to
the end of the bowsprit, others to the end of the jib-boom. In
bad weather they had preventive-braces that led aft to the rail.
She carried fore-topmast staysail, jib and flying-jib."

Regardless of the many and varied claims put forth by the
men who built and sailed them, all these smart little vessels,

with their different and often outlandish rigs, produced results — and that counted, on the Maine Coast or anywhere else.

☆ ☆ ☆

Pirates had always infested the waters of the West Indies, but those of the 1820's were particularly obnoxious, with a special hate for Mainers.

In November of 1821, eleven pirate craft were cruising off the southeast coast of Cuba. Their crews were not the brave, hard-fighting men of Henry Morgan's day, or even of Rackham's or Stede Bonnet's. These were sneaky and mean cutthroats; low-caste Spaniards, half-breeds, Indians and Negroes. They didn't murder and torture in the way of business; their crimes were committed for the pleasure of making others suffer.

Many of the scoundrels operated close to shore, in small boats, the crews living in caves. They gave no quarter, yet, like all cowards, when the positions were reversed, expected it.

In August of 1821, the Nobleboro brig *Dolphin* was overtaken and successfully boarded. The mate was stabbed to death, the other members of the brig's company hoisted by the neck and otherwise tortured, until they told where the money was hidden, then hanged for real.

The next January, this same gang of bloodthirsty wretches captured the *Alliance* of Kennebunk. All aboard were stripped and set adrift naked in a small boat, without food or water, after having been beaten and tortured. The crews of the *Evergreen, Mary Jane, Dispatch* and *Milo* were given the same treatment.

The *Cobbseconte* was taken four miles off Morro Castle. Its Maine crew was stripped, some set adrift, while the more favored had a line fastened around their waists and were tossed overboard, where they were dragged astern until devoured piecemeal by the swarming sharks.

The Portland brig *Mechanic* was burned and the entire crew murdered, horribly.

The *Belisarius* brig of Kennebunk, under command of Captain Clement Perkins, was sighted by a pirate schooner of forty-odd tons, off Campeche. Unarmed, the Mainer ran for it, but was overtaken, boarded, the officers and crew bound hand and foot. The pirate captain stood before Perkins. "The money, senor."

Captain Perkins told where it was located. Disappointed by the small amount they found, the pirates showed their resentment on the Kennebunk master's person. First they cut off his right arm, then his left. They cut off both legs above the knees. Still not satisfied, they filled his mouth with oakum which had been saturated in oil, then set it on fire.

Americans up to now had realized that something ugly was going on, with vessels and their entire crews vanishing without trace, but it was the capture of the brig *Betsy* that led to the pirates' demise. All the crew was murdered bar one who escaped.

He carried his terrible tale back to Maine where it evoked such an uproar that America embarked on an official campaign of extinction in which they were eagerly assisted by the British.

The navies of the two nations, working together, wiped the pirates from the sea then set about firing their shore nests. The infamous bands that had given no quarter received none. Furthermore, combined British and American landing parties on Cuban soil took into custody Spaniards who had been acting as agents for the pirates, and helping them in other ways. These miscreants likewise never went to trial but were ruthlessly exterminated for the vermin that they were.

Although the commerce with the Islands had been slow to revive, now, with the ridding of the pirate menace, it began to improve. As time went on, the larger merchants established business connections with their opposites in the West Indies and this gave assurance of a regular market and for return cargoes. But it was not until the Roaring Forties that trade really boomed.

Chapter Five

THE ROARING FORTIES

THESE WERE THE years of great activity. The country as a whole was awakening to its vast potentials, and in the Maine ports it seemed that the awakening was even more so. Leastwise, it seemed to be more bustling and noisier.

New Hampshire men, who had through the long years made a point of not fully appreciating the worth of Maine and Mainers, now apparently saw the light, and brought their produce down from beyond the White Mountains through Crawford Notch. From the former Hampshire Grants came Vermonters using the same route.

In long trains of red pungs, they trailed over the frozen winter roads, bringing hogs, butter and lard to barter for the West India goods; rum, coffee, sugar and molasses leading all the rest. The rum imports, however, slackened off when Mainers saw the advantage of distilling their own. Soon there were seven distilleries going full blast in Portland, plus others along the coast. Vaughan's great establishment in Hallowell was said to be one of the largest in the United States. During one winter a Pittston store sold locally ninety hogsheads. And after the Cumberland and Oxford Canal was in operation, a single bargee reported that in one season he delivered three hundred barrels to the various towns. Multiply this by at least a hundred boatmen, and you have something.

Coffee was the favored cargo, not especially for its value but because it was clean and easy to handle. Cuba, at first, and later Haiti, produced the bulk, then Brazil came in and made Rio the principal coffee port.

The varied trade in West India goods inspired allied industries that brought additional income to Maine; coopering and construction of sugar boxes, shooks, lumber and so on. More mills were set up to handle the requirements, and the shipyards were busy turning off brigs and other craft.

[29]

Although sugar was an important import, it sold in huge white cones for the luxury trade. Brown sugar, raw, was for the ordinary folks, and what was known as "muscovado" was obtained by draining molasses through holes in the hogshead bottoms after crystallization had begun.

The sharp-minded Portland merchants soon decided that profits could be made from the local refining of raw sugar. John Bundy Brown, the first, after much experimenting developed a process that produced quality sugar that could be sold at reasonable prices. He incorporated his Portland Sugar House in 1855, a sprawling establishment eight stories high, with warehouses and wharves, and employment of two hundred persons. Its capacity was two hundred fifty barrels a day, and thirty hogsheads of molasses a year.

Yes, business was booming in Maine and everywhere. Banks were organized, and insurance companies, shipping firms and newspapers. The tall ships began to make their appearance, most of them full-bodied until the demand of the Forty-niners called for speed. It was a time when Maine boys who had never been anywhere, except possibly to the West Indies, went everywhere.

The very air of Maine was charged with the urge to be up and doing; the Big Men to accomplish great projects, the lesser folk and youngsters to start up the first rung of the ladder.

When John Agry built his first bark at Hallowell in 1828, and launched her as the *Caroline,* Alvalvah Knox was among the spectators. He was so taken by the vessel that he signed on for her maiden voyage.

Alvalvah was a Waldo County boy, who had strayed, or lost his way, and wound up on the Kennebec. And as long as he had left home and got so far, he saw no reason to tarry. The new bark offered opportunity for travel, inasmuch as she was about to enter the cotton trade.

In the South, cotton production had more than doubled in the decade from 1820 to 1830. As more than four-fifths of the crop was consigned to the British Isles or Europe, vessels and crewmen were needed in proportion to the unprecedented demand.

On this first voyage, or possibly it was the second, the *Caroline* put into New York Harbor to take on some necessary gear. While she was berthed at South Street, Alvalvah thought to see the sights of the big city.

A six-footer and rugged, he was also the serious type, and in his spare time was studying for the ministry. As a sort of by-product of his study and inclination he was a do-gooder, always ready and willing to help, even insisting on it, whether his assistance was wanted or not, with results that were often embarrassing.

So the Maine boy strolled up Broadway and towards the East Side, minded to see the Bowery he'd heard so much about. Finally, at a place where five streets came together, he saw a heavy-set man standing under a lamppost. What attracted Alvalvah's attention to him in the first place was the fact that although his garments were worn to being on the shabby side, the fellow sported a gray bowler hat, a fancy vest and carried a heavy walking stick.

Alvalvah didn't know it, but he was looking at a member of the famous gang called "Plug Uglies" who had wandered into the territory controlled by the "Five Point Gang." Therefore, he was somewhat shocked when two rough looking characters accosted Fancy Vest and beat him to the flagging, with what looked like bean bags, only larger.

He started off to find a policeman when he spied a handsomely dressed gentleman standing in a doorway, smiling at the little drama unfolding under the lamppost. "Can't we do something?" he asked.

"I wouldn't advise it," the gentleman said, flicking a spot of dust from his sleeve with a silk handkerchief, before taking a pair of brass knuckles from his pocket and slipping them on. "Even a Sparrow should know better than that," the Bowery Boy added.

Alvalvah wondered why his friendly advisor called him a "Sparrow," and he was inclined to resent it, but just then several of the victim's friends joined the struggle across the street, armed with what were definitely blackjacks. Then more Five Pointers came running, armed with their beanbags (actually sand bags, used because they left no mark, while giving a victim concussion, or bringing about his death).

Soon a full-fledged Donnybrook was in progress, with no
sight of a cop, except the not too distant banging of a night-
stick against the flagging. He resolved then and there to break
up the fight himself.

He squared his broad shoulders and marched across the
street. He shoved his way into the middle of the brawlers.
"Break it up, boys," he ordered.

There was an instant pause in the conflict. The combatants
stared at the Sparrow who walked in where Angels and the
Police feared to tread. "The fight's over," Alvalvah added.

He couldn't have been more wrong.

☆   ☆   ☆

The mate of the *Caroline* was checking his cargo when he
was startled to see a battle-marked procession wending its way
down the dock, bearing a bloodied bundle of rags. It halted by
the Maine bark. Two delegates of the three gangs detached
themselves from the party to go back and examine the name-
plate.

"This is her, then," the spokesman said. "Hey, Cull," he
called to the mate. "We've brot back your sailor boy. Sorry
for what happened, but we didn't suspect he was a foreigner.
We thot he was a Jersey Sparrow."

☆   ☆   ☆

Like Alvalvah Knox, Mainers in the old days were willing
to try anything once as long as there was a prospect of some
profit. Therefore, after reading and hearing of the successful
whaling voyages by the fleets of Provincetown, New Bedford,
Nantucket and Fairhaven, they reasoned that if nowadays whale
oil was where the money lay, why should Massachusetts men be
allowed to skim the cream without the benefit of their experience
in seamanship, fishing and commercial shrewdness?

Some Maine boys did go down to the Bay State and sign on
aboard a whaler, but the Money Men wanted to invest and felt
soundly snubbed when their offers of cash backing were
laughed at. The whaling people didn't need outside capital;
they were making plenty, and not inclined to share it.

Disappointed, the investors trooped back to Maine, the
cash still in their pockets. Most were from Wiscasset; dissatis-

fied merchants and shipowners, who yearned for the good old days when they had been top men in the region.

A number of meetings were subsequently held at which it was agreed that opportunity was not only knocking, she was pounding at the door. So the Wiscasset Whale Fishing Company was organized, committees appointed to further the project and one to find a suitable ship.

A hull on the ways of the Hitchcock yard at Damariscotta was purchased and towed to Wiscasset to be finished and rigged out as a whaler. When it was done she was christened the *Wiscasset* and sent off to the distant whaling grounds under the command of Captain Richard Macy.

He was an experienced whaler and returned forty months later with 2,800 barrels of sperm oil, enough to repay the Company for the cost of the ship and clear all the bills, but not sufficient to warrant a dividend for the shareholders.

Refitted, the ship sailed again to return after two and a half years with 900 barrels of sperm, $6,517 in cash and 150 pounds of coffee. Sperm oil was then selling at a dollar per gallon and the venture had therefore proved profitable, but for some reason the Company became discouraged and the sturdy *Wiscasset* was sold.

☆　☆　☆

A launching was always a red letter day, drawing crowds from far and near. The village schools were closed, refreshment stands spotted in likely places and everyone good natured.

In general liquor flowed rather freely; perhaps too freely on a launching at Brewer, on the Penobscot.

This was the launching of the 599-ton ship *James M. Littlefield* from the Cooper Yard. Proud of their achievement, the owners and builders decided to make the occasion a memorable one, with considerable speechmaking combined with what was afterwards claimed to be only a mild liquid celebration.

When the big moment finally arrived, the top of the ways and the bottom of the slides greased with softsoap and tallow, and enough flaxseed to hold it in place, the experts took their sledges and iron wedges then went beneath the ship's bottom.

They started about half an hour before flood, working in pairs from stern toward the bows as they split out the heavy blocks on which the keel rested. They had need to be alert, ready to jump at the first creak, and with the first splintering crackle of rushing timber they did.

Up to now everything had gone off smoothly and orthodox, but to make more of a presentation the people in charge had arranged to launch the little *Littlefield* fully rigged and gay with bunting. Shoreside, a brass band added to the din, its clamor rising above the roar of the multitude. On board the deck was crowded with top-hatted, frock-coated dignitaries, their ladies in best gowns and bonnets.

To avoid a chance of accident the ship's port anchor was swung free, and it was dropped to snub her as she left the ways. Evidently it was dropped too soon for it took hold with a jerk that gave her a sharp list and slid those on deck in a wild tangle of arm and leg waving, and feminine screams, to port with her.

This panicked throng, combined with the list and the weight of the topmasts and backing yards, capsized the vessel with the result that the elite of two cities were hurled into the water, tophats, beribboned bonnets and all.

No lives were lost that apparently counted in that era, the Bangor paper reporting that "only one Irishman was drowned." Who he was, or what he was doing in Brewer or whether he had left a family of mites fatherless was not considered important enough to recount.

The *Littlefield* was later righted, cleaned out and refitted where necessary and sailed the seas profitably for her owners until August 14, 1864 when, at 42:20 N – 66 W, she was sunk by the Confederate raider *Tallahassee*.

☆   ☆   ☆

From the beginning of shipbuilding in Maine, it had been the custom to christen a vessel with a bottle of rum, and following the launching large quantities of that same beverage would be consumed by guests, invited and otherwise.

It was therefore an unhappy day when in 1837 General James Appleton of Portland became concerned with what he regarded as a situation which had reached saturation point.

He applied his parade ground voice and the weight of his rank to the advocation of State-wide prohibition. Although this was a long time coming, the Temperance Movement found a ready reception and was soon recruiting hordes to its cause. Crowds who might earlier have attended festivities at which the spirits flowed, in this period began turning to rallies which were purely spiritual.

Converts steadily grew in number, persistently petitioning the Legislature until in 1846 that worthy body, overawed by the mounting pressure of public opinion, enacted a law prohibiting the sale of alcoholic liquors except for medicinal and mechanical purposes. This was the famous — or infamous, depending on how you look at it — Maine Law, the first of its kind in the United States.

To the advocates of freedom there was still a faint gleam of hope: that the law might be declared unconstitutional. To find out they hired lawyers who took the case to the Supreme Court of the United States.

Meanwhile, the law in Maine was not yet effective but gave time to make the most of dwindling supplies. And they were indeed dwindling, with those that could afford it stocking up against the black day when they would no longer be able to buy in a bottle or two of grog when they wanted.

The reformers had gained such a thorough hold in the state that in many yards ships were no longer sent down the ways in the time-honored manner. At launchings rum gave way to water, and as if to rub salt into the wound of the diehards it became the custom to hold a religious ceremony before the blocks were split out. The Stetson yard at Camden was said to be the first to go dry, but at Kennebunk they really went to extremes. There, on the Sunday before a vessel sailed and on the Sabbath after the vessel returned from its voyage, the entire ship's crew and officers would attend church services in a body.

And when the *Benjamin Sewall,* the largest and last vessel to be launched at Brunswick's Pennel yard was sent down the ways, a thousand turned out to listen to the address by General Joshua Chamberlain, President of Bowdoin College, following which they joined in prayer with Professor John S. Sewall before a bottle of spring water was broken across the ship's bows and she took off.

Quite a change indeed from the old-style launchings when a rum cask might be broke out for the crowd.

☆ ☆ ☆

In the spring of 1837, a Rockland Limer, the schooner *Susan,* Captain Daniel Philbrook of Camden, worked her way down the Atlantic coast to Savannah, Georgia. Her mate was Edward Kelleran of Cushing and her crew Knox County men and boys.

The *Susan* discharged her cargo of lime and her company breathed a sigh of relief, for the vessel had been leaking badly, a danger when carrying this product. She was then put into drydock for repairs to the hull.

A recommended local shipwright was engaged for the job. Although James Sagurs wasn't at all partial to Yankees or Abolitionists, both of which the ship's company were, he was not above taking their money. It was one of his workmen who came close to starting the Civil War twenty-four years ahead of time.

Atticus was his name, and he was an expert carpenter. But he was also a slave. Making friends with the crew and plying them with questions concerning working and living conditions in the North he was obviously impressed by their glowing word pictures. "Your state must be close to Heaven," he said once.

It was later claimed by the South and denied by the North that Atticus thereupon announced his intention to flee Georgia for Maine, where a man might be free, treated fairly and even get an education.

The repairs completed, Captain Philbrook paid off James Sagurs, got his clearance papers and sailed the *Susan* out of Savannah harbor. A few days later, well up the coast, Atticus, the twenty-two year old Negro slave, was discovered a stowaway in the forward hold among some casks.

The schooner had come too far to turn back so it continued on its course. Philbrook, the mate and crew were all favorably impressed with the boy and promised to find him work in Maine at his trade. Already suspicious however when his slave did not report for work at the usual time, Sagurs put two and two together, and determined that no Yank would steal his property no matter what the cost of recovering it.

He thereupon chartered the fastest pilot boat he could find and gave chase to the *Susan*, blood in his heart and two Navy revolvers in his waistband.

The schooner wasn't built for racing, but nor did she know she was being chased, yet she reached Rockland, then called East Thomaston well ahead of pursuit. The crewmen scattered to their homes and Ed Kelleran, the mate, took the runaway slave to his home in Cushing.

When Sagurs arrived in port he was in an absolute fury. Informed of the supposed whereabouts of the slave he secured a warrant for arrest which was given to Deputy Sheriff D. N. Piper to serve. He promptly hitched up his team and drove to the Kelleran farm, where no trace could be found of Atticus, who had already been whisked off elsewhere.

The Deputy in turn went through the other houses in Cushing, missing only the one where the boy was hiding. As the hunt went on, Sagurs' rage and frustration grew until he was vowing to "skin that boy alive."

His next step was to post a reward of twenty dollars for information leading to the slave's capture, but as the people of Cushing felt only sympathy for the slave who wanted to be a Mainer he might have remained in the village indefinitely had it not been for two local boys who put the reward above principle. Not only did they inform the authorities as to the whereabouts of Atticus, they added treachery to their greed.

They went to Atticus posing as friends who wished to help him out of his dilemma and told him that the "Underground Railway," the name given to the organization working to free the slaves, had a station at Thomaston. They added that a large group of ex-slaves lived on the Knox estate and that he would be safe there.

Atticus, who had encountered only sympathy and honesty in Maine, believed them and, unbeknown to Kelleran who was absent at the time, accompanied the Judas pair to where he thought his freedom lay. But it was the Law and Sagurs who were in wait and he was promptly handcuffed like a common criminal, taken to Rockland, given a severe beating by his master and put aboard the pilot boat heavily ironed. Next morning it sailed for Savannah.

James Sagurs the shipwright had his property back, and it can only be imagined the life that the slave who had caused him so much trouble led when he got back, if indeed he lived at all. But the beatings to which the slave was subjected did little to appease Sagurs who on his return to home soil swore out a complaint against Philbrook and Kelleran and caused to be despatched two Georgia officers to go North to take them into custody.

In Rockland the officers were told that the wanted men were off on an "extended fishing trip" and had to return empty handed. Disappointed in this attempt at vengeance, Sagurs next put the matter up to Governor William Schley of Georgia asking him to intervene in the interest of "justice." Schley was not particularly taken with the idea, but finally, on June 21, 1837 despatched a letter to Governor Dunlap of Maine demanding that both mariners be arrested as "fugitives from Georgia justice," and turned over to agent Mordecai Sheftall to be brought back for trial.

The Maine governor was not pleased with this high and mighty demand, knowing full well what kind of "justice" Philbrook and Kelleran, two highly respected citizens, might expect in Georgia: they would wind up on a chain-gang doing hard labor. He waited before replying in the hope that by then hot tempers might have cooled, until the following August when he sent back a refusal.

Governor Schley was taken aback. He had not been too interested at first, but now he was riled and the Georgian public also was aroused.

"Close Southern ports to Maine shipping," one newspaper headline shouted.

"Arrest all Mainers found on the sacred soil of Georgia," another declared, adding that they be held as hostages until Philbrook and Kelleran were given up.

Eventually the Georgia Legislature declared by resolution that Dunlap's refusal was not only dangerous to Georgia's rights but a "direct violation of the Federal Constitution."

Copies were sent to the President, members of Congress and the governors of all the states. A challenge to Maine to virtually submit or take the consequences, it was one of the earliest pronouncements of States Rights.

Georgia next secured an indictment against the Maine men, a copy of which was sent to Governor Kent, successor to Dunlap, who also sent back a flat refusal to arrest the pair.

In retaliation the Georgia governor demanded that any Mainer who came "within the jurisdiction of Georgia, on board a vessel as owner, officer, or mariner, be considered as doing so with the intent of committing the crime of seducing Negro slaves from their rightful owners." The said Mainers were to be dealt with accordingly, he added.

The Georgia Legislature did not act on this wild proposal, but nonetheless Maine ships gave Georgia a wide berth for many years thereafter.

Chapter Six

CALIFORNIA — HERE WE COME

IT IS A FACT that all through the history of the United States, whenever an event of national importance was taking place, or in the making, Mainers were there! And often as not, they were the cause of it.

When on a fine spring day in 1848, the quiet of the siesta hour of the little California town of San Francisco was rudely shattered by the sound of pounding hoofbeats and hoarse-throated warwhoops, dozing citizens started up, grabbed their muskets and streamed into the open, certain that the redskins had risen.

It was a single horseman who sent his lathered mount onto the old Plaza and circled it three times, standing in the stirrups while "yellerin' 'n' bellerin' fit-to-kill." A giant, rugged and broad-beamed, long hair and shaggy beard flying and travel-dusted, as were his garments, he drew rein. Eyes gleaming wildly, he shook an old horseradish bottle before the startled faces of the crowd. "Gold!" he roared, shaking the bottle again, so that the yellow sand and nuggets gleamed in the sunlight. "Gold from the American River!"

The noisy giant was now recognized as Sam Brennan, of Saco, Maine, manager of Captain John Sutter's store, at his settlement near Sacramento. It was the indiscreet enthusiasm of the Man from Maine that resulted in the Great Gold Rush of 1849!

☆ ☆ ☆

There was almost instant action when the news of the great strike appeared in the Maine newspapers of September of 1848. The greatest stampede occurred at Bath, where 19 vessels left for San Francisco before the end of 1849. Portland and Bangor each sent 13, Eastport 10, Belfast 3 in addition to occasional craft from smaller towns. In all, sixty-seven vessels cleared Maine ports jam-packed with fortune-seekers, and a total of

775 cleared Atlantic seaboard harbors that one year bound for the land of golden promise.

The first Maine vessel to sail was the bark *Suliot*, only recently launched, which cleared Belfast with a very mixed company indeed, including loggers, mechanics, merchants, farmers, a dentist, a printer, a hatter and a lawyer. There was also a surveyor and some who signed on as "gentlemen."

The cargo was in keeping; about everything usable and so diversified that the manifest was fifteen feet long. The cargo even included what might have been the forerunners of the prefabricated housing industry: small houses that had been knocked down by their owners to be erected thousands of miles away.

Preparations for the long voyage caused considerable excitement on the banks of the Penobscot, and on the Saturday night before sailing a great banquet was held, with a long speakers table and Governor Anderson of Maine presiding.

The speeches promised a prosperous future for California now that Mainers were on their way to take over. In addition to the gold there were bountiful natural resources, and it would be these resources that the thrift and enterprise of the New Englanders would develop, the speakers declared.

The listening adventurers paid scant attention to this good advice. Were they going to farm, log and suchlike while others reaped a harvest of golden nuggets? Not likely.

January 30 was bitter cold but that did not faze a huge and enthusiastic crowd from gathering to see the bark sail. A minister was on hand to preach a parting sermon and a band to play the vessel into the bay, but it was so cold that the bass horns were all but helpless.

Off the ship sailed finally until after a passage of some 171 days she arrived at San Francisco. The month was July, hot and hazy, and many of the company struck out immediately for the goldfields while the merchants set up shop. The most profitable of all the cargo ventures were hemlock boards. Bought in Belfast at ten dollars per thousand feet, they sold in San Francisco for three hundred per thousand!

☆ ☆ ☆

The *Andrew Scott* of only 318 tons burthen was not the first vessel away from Maine in 1849, but she had the distinction of being the first full-rigged ship to carry Forty-niners round the Horn.

Her project was financed by a group of Portland business-men. Lumber, they had been informed, was selling at a pre-mium on the Pacific coast, San Francisco being an especially good market. With lumber now up to four hundred dollars per thousand feet, it didn't take much of a mathematician to reach a very happy estimate of the profits waiting inside the Golden Gate.

Maine builders and shipowners and masters had never pre-viously given too much thought to the time element in delivering a cargo, being satisfied that it was delivered safely in a time that whatever conditions happened to prevail made possible.

Making her way steadfastly round the Horn, the *Andrew Scott* reached San Francisco in May of 1850 — only to find that she had been too slow and the bottom had dropped out of the lumber market. All was not quite lost, however, for the *Scott's* master, William Leavitt, had played it safe when loading and had taken aboard a small two-masted sailboat, the *Naumkeag*.

The sailboat which cost the captain one hundred eighty dollars sold for a tidy two thousand. He had struck the right market at the right moment, for freight rates between San Francisco and Sacramento were running from sixty to one hundred twenty dollars per ton. The demand, therefore, for any easy to handle, small sailing craft was great. Nor did the new owners of the *Naumkeag* have reason to regret their investment, for she cleared a profit of six hundred to a thou-sand dollars per week.

The fact that the *Scott*, by reason of her slowness, lost the high lumber market was something for Maine to think over. And thinking on the problem forged the key that opened the door on the clipper era.

The *Scott's* passage had taken one hundred sixty days. Had she been able to do it in one hundred ten, or better, her Portland backers would have gained a small fortune.

It was obvious to the eastern businessman and shipowner that speed in delivery of passengers and freight was essential. Owners were no longer their own shippers; they could make more money by rendering carrier service to the merchants. The merchants on their part insisted that the goods reach destination in the shortest possible time.   Paying eighty dollars a ton freight, they wanted results.

The ship designers were aware that an altogether different model was required to meet the current demand.   Their thoughts turned back to the topsail schooner of the old days, with her high, sharp bows.   To obtain speed, high, sharp bows were the ticket, but it would be at the expense of cargo space. To offset this lack, the walking freight (passengers) and the exceptionally high rates paid for the regular freight lessened the importance of capacity.   So from the drawing boards the clipper ships evolved and rapidly came into production.

Chapter Seven

THE SHARP SHIPS

MAINE HAD LED the United States in the building of ships since the opening forties, but her designers and builders felt an odd reluctance in taking up with the new models. It was not that they had any objection to speed; they knew that to be necessary under the modern conditions. Furthermore, they had shown appreciation of its value in the topsail schooners and fast little brigs. But it bothered them to do away with cargo space, even a square foot.

The way they looked at it, this present big money economy was only a boom. Some day the boom would be over, and the shipping industry would be overstocked with handsome, fast ships that couldn't carry enough cargo to pay expenses. As events would prove, they were right.

Still, there was a powerful market for fast ships, and no reason at all why they shouldn't be in on it, so they set to work on the problem and came up with the sharp-built ships known as the State of Maine Clippers. Construction began in 1850 and lasted four years. By 1856, just as the Maine men had feared, the demand dwindled almost to vanishing point.

Metcalf and Norris of Damariscotta were the pioneer clipper builders in Maine. Their 1,713-ton *Flying Scud* was probably the most famous. An extremely sharp clipper, in an extremely sharp class, she was built with speed in mind. The fourth of five record-breaking Maine clippers, she was launched in the summer of 1853. So rapidly did she pass down the river that her officers could hardly believe it possible. In fact, they were certain that the chronometers were out of order, and it took a deal of checking for them to realize that it wasn't so.

Hardly had the *Flying Scud* arrived in New York when she was purchased by H. W. Cameron for his Australian Pioneer Line. His advertising slogan was "Sixty days to Melbourne."

The Maine clipper sailed on September 9th, under command of Captain William H. Bearce, who was determined to live up to the firm's slogan.

It wasn't to be; not on this maiden voyage. In the Gulf
Stream the *Flying Scud* was struck by lightning which completely magnetized the cargo of ore in her after hold. This af-
fected the compasses, the needles whirling like mad, and therefore useless.

Finally, Yankee ingenuity solved the problem. The compass was fastened to a long board that was extended over the
port side, away from the influence of the cargo. It made for
an awkward reading but was better than none at all.

Aside from compass trouble, the *Scud* was overloaded so
that her scuppers were nearly awash. Added to this, she was
trimmed by the head two feet and this made her very cranky.
Yet she did make the passage in seventy-six days.

A notation was made in her log on November 6th that has
been the subject of maritime argument ever since, and grows
stronger with the years. On that day Captain Bearce wrote,
"the *Flying Scud* ran four hundred and forty-nine nautical
miles," a statement, if it could be substantiated, that would
indicate the best day's run for any clipper. Unfortunately the
log book is not available.

"Captain Bearce made a mistake in his reckoning," the dissident element argues. "It's happened before."

To those who knew Bearce this was considered highly improbable. He wasn't given to errors in navigation. So to this
day Maine's claim to the fastest sailing ship passage of all time
is a matter for dispute.

Two of her outstanding passages were from New York to
Marseilles in under twenty days, and from Marseilles to Bombay
in eighty-one. The Bombay passage set a record, beaten later
by only three days.

On November 30, 1853, Trufant and Drummond launched
their second fast ship of that year, the *Viking*, with a sea rover
in armor for a figurehead. Her best run was 108 days to California in 1858.

Mainers could build fast ships when they set their minds
to it.

☆   ☆   ☆

The Maine shipyards turned out thirty-three clippers at
the peak of the "speed boom," twenty-four over one thousand
tons. Of these, five launched in 1853 made the passage to San

Francisco in under 110 days. In 1857, the Bath clipper *Flying Dragon* did it in ninety-seven days.

The other fast Maine clippers were all "extreme"; the *Dashing Wave, Spitfire, Viking* and *Oracle*.

The *Red Jacket* was probably the most famous of all the Maine clippers, and one of the more beautiful. She was large too, for a clipper, 2,306 tons.

Built by Deacon Thomas in his Rockland yard, the *Red Jacket,* named after the Iroquois chief, was designed by Samuel Hart Pook and was as near perfect as a ship could be. Extreme as the most extreme from the Boston yards, she was trim and sharp, with a delicate beauty in her graceful lines and high stem, matched by finely proportioned spars and standing rigging. Her figurehead was a life-sized carving of the great Seneca, and her light, carefully modeled stern held a bust of the same severe Indian, surrounded by heavy gilt scrollwork.

Furnishings inboard and outboard were of the best quality. Done in rosewood mahogany, satin and zebra wood the after cabin was enhanced by a trim of black walnut and giltwork. It held fourteen staterooms within the forward cabin, exclusive of officers' quarters. The forecastle accommodated a crew of eighty-two.

Towed to New York a week after launching, she was there given masts and spars, was rigged and her sails bent. On January 10th, after a much advertised maiden voyage, she sailed for Liverpool.

Everything was against even a fair passage. Uncoppered, her crew untrained, most of them lubbers, the drawbacks were offset by a master, Captain Asa Eldridge, who knew his business and who was fortunate in his officers. So despite foul weather nearly every day of the passage, with hail, rain or snow or a combination of all three, the *Red Jacket* arrived in Liverpool on January 23rd. Her time from dock to dock was 13 days, 1 hour and 25 minutes, a record that still stands for sailing ships.

On six consecutive days her runs averaged 343 nautical miles. After that her average wasn't so good, although on the ninth day for the twenty-four hour run she logged 413 nautical miles. That was when the crew "spliced the main brace" to celebrate to such an extent that the watches were short-handed for forty-eight hours.

The arrival of the clipper in Liverpool was highly dramatic. Huge crowds were on hand to greet the big American ship. Ignoring the waiting tugs, the *Red Jacket* swept up the Mersey under full sail, in a brisk northwester, and fairly boiled up to the pier. It was then that Captain Eldridge accomplished a feat seldom attempted. The ship came about, threw her yards aback and laid herself up to the pierhead with a precision that brought a roar of approval from the spectators.

It was in 1853 that the high-water mark was reached in the enthusiasm for clippers. The freight rates were still high, with speed of paramount importance. So everybody was building the big, fast ships and everybody seemed to be sailing them. Times were good and apparently they were going to stay that way.

Even the Maine builders, long given to over-caution, began to wonder if maybe they hadn't been wrong about the clippers, but not the Prophets of Doom. They knew better, but no busy person ever gave any heed to their dire warnings. Yet even without the Prophets to point them out, the signs were there for the discerning eye. Commercial depression was bound to follow so many boom years, and there was ominous indication that a humdinger was building up, although still distant like the thin purple haze of a fog bank on the horizon.

In 1853, therefore, more than half the total tonnage of the entire clipper fleet was built. Nor was it difficult to raise the money to build a clipper. Every person with capital to invest fought to buy shares in such a project.

In Maine the yards specializing in this type of vessel, and they were but four, put off thirty-three. And while the majority did not have the speed of the Outlander product, five, as already stated, compared with the best that the famous clipper pioneer Donald McKay of Boston had to offer.

The *Flying Dragon* was the fastest. Built by Trufant and Drummond of Bath, she was the only Maine vessel to make the run from Boston round the Horn to San Francisco in less than one hundred days. She did it in ninety-seven. Over a five-year period she was able to average the fifteen thousand mile run in 112 3/5 days. In 1860 she made the passage from Sydney, Australia to Hampton Roads in seventy-five days, a record run.

Maine's *Spitfire* was a close second to the *Flying Dragon* in the matter of speed. An extreme clipper, she was launched in 1853 by James Arey and Sons at Frankfort, and she was commanded by John Arey, who wasn't exactly a driver. However, he had a mate who was. Elkanah Crowell wasn't truly a Bucko, but he was able to pass for one.

Mister Crowell is credited with the remark that he "wished no man in his crew who could not jump over the foreyard before breakfast."

Evidently he found four who couldn't. When the ship put into Rio, after sailing from Boston in October, he discharged them for "incompetence."

That the others profited by this example is also evident, for the *Spitfire* arrived in San Francisco only 120 days out of Boston, despite losing two weeks in the gales off the Horn. This made her actual sailing time a few hours under one hundred days. Her best record was in 1860 when racing the California course with the *Black Hawk*. They both made it in 107 days.

The Kittery firm of Fernald and Pettigrew built the third fastest Maine clipper, the *Dashing Wave*. Sailing from Boston on January 1, 1858, she too made the California run in 107 days. And she had the distinction of being the last clipper in active service. In 1920, when sixty-two years old, her hull when examined was found to be in sound condition, a tribute to the fine material and workmanship that went into the State of Maine Clippers.

☆   ☆   ☆

The first of the three clippers built in 1850 in the Maine yards was the *Alert,* by Metcalf and Norris of Damariscotta. At the time of her launching not a soul had an inkling that she was going to be a clipper, because she was neither extreme nor exactly sharp either. But in light of later performance she earned the honor.

Launched in November, the *Alert* was promptly sent to New York to take part in the Gold Rush trade. From this port she sailed December 29th under command of Captain Francis Bursley and the blue and yellow house flag of Crocker and Warren.

Aside from being the first, the small Maine clipper had one other possible claim to fame; as the ship that knew the first

Maine Bucko Mate, although Ira Cutts wasn't a true Bucko of the type that developed in the Down Easter era.

Mister Cutts was a Downeaster who held strong opinions, especially on the matter of food, and even more especially when it came to the preparation of that Downeast delicacy known as soggy dumplings.

Milo Hentz the cook, from Portland, had equally strong opinions, particularly when they involved the products of his profession. And it was on just such a trivial matter that there developed between the two a feud that made the mate a butt for seafaring humor up and down the coast of Maine.

"Dumplings should be light and fluffy, the way I make them," Milo maintained. "The other kind, the way you want them, are only fit for hogs."

Mister Cutts paled with rage. "Are you daring to insinuate that I am a hog?" he roared.

"You said it, I didn't," Milo grinned as he went into the galley and closed the door, only opening it to add, "Sir," before closing it again.

The mate took the matter to the Captain who considered it with the judicial calm of a Solomon. "Can't you make allowances, Mister?" he asked. "You know how temperamental cooks are, and this is a good one."

"Sir, no cook is good who won't make soggy dumplings. I surmise this one doesn't know how. That is what is behind his contrary stand."

"Why can't you take regular dumplings and pour water on them?" the Old Man suggested. "That will make them soggy as all get-out."

Mister Cutts took a step backward, as if he had been struck in the face. "You can't be serious, sir?"

"Why not?" the Captain asked stubbornly. "Everybody else wants fluffy dumplings, and the cook makes good ones." He paused and smacked his lips. "I believe we're due for some tonight. If you want yours soggy, pour water over them. It's simple as that."

"Thank you, sir. I won't bother you any further over such a trivial matter." He turned on his heel and headed purposefully for the break, went down the ladder and marched toward the galley. The Captain watched his progress with some concern. There was something about the set of Mister Cutts' broad shoulders he didn't like.

☆ ☆ ☆

On January 11, 1851, just two weeks after the *Alert* left New York for the Pacific Coast, she was followed by the *Grey Feather*. Eastport-built by C. S. Husten, the *Feather* was sleek as a smelt, with a sail plan that would soon take her into the ranks of the record-breakers under two Downeast masters; Captain Daniel McLaughlin, a native of Grand Manan, and Captain Bartlett Mayo of Hampden.

It was under McLaughlin that the *Grey Feather* made her famed 1854 run from Melbourne to Calcutta in thirty-six days. Under Mayo she made a passage of fourteen thousand miles from New York to Australia in eighty-four days.

The *Grey Feather*, a full-modeled 586-tonner, was, however, close to being an extreme clipper, as different from the eleven other craft that were built in Maine in 1851 and designated clippers, although they actually weren't. Limited by their background and training, the Mainers simply could not bring themselves to give up seemingly undue amounts of cargo space for passenger cabins. Instead of the extreme clippers they built modified ones. The lines looked sharp, and most of the ships turned off were, but the cargo and passenger space was about equally divided, for the shipbuilders had not been able to go at it wholeheartedly merely for speed and record passages.

As the call for speed and more speed grew ever louder, the Maine builders gradually began to respond to the challenge. George Thomas of Rockland set off the little *Springbok*, a lively bark that in miniature was a forerunner of the *Red Jacket*. At Bath, Trufant and Drummond, with the launching of the *Monsoon* started what was to be a famous fleet. The beautiful *Snow Squall* was turned off at South Portland; at Kittery's historic Badger's Island, Fernald and Pettigrew launched the *Typhoon*. Most important of all, up the river at Eliot, at Green Acre, Samuel Hanscom built that masterpiece of marine construction, the lovely *Nightingale*.

☆ ☆ ☆

The extreme clipper *Nightingale*, like some people, was born for adventure, and she had a long life of it; nearly half a century. A beautiful ship and named for Jenny Lind, whose likeness was carved in her figurehead, to sailors and landsmen alike she was as glamorous as the lady herself.

It was in June, 1851, that she was launched from Samuel Hanscom's South Eliot yard, a tall-masted, high-bowed, sharp ship designed on the lines of a yacht by the builder's nephew, Isaiah Hanscom. She was not intended for the Cape Horn trade, but for the passenger luxury runs to the World's Fair in London. Fitted out with luxurious saloons and staterooms, between decks she was more like one of the plush hotels of the era, although this had no effect on her sailing ability.

All clippers cost a deal of money, but Sam had gone overboard in building the *Nightingale*. Heavily mortgaged, she was sent to Boston for sale. Bid in by the ship brokers, Sampson and Tappan who paid seventy-five thousand dollars for her, she sailed for some years under the house flag of that concern, white over blue centered by a red ball. The owners were proud of her and offered to race any British or American ship to China for a stake of ten thousand pounds, a challenge that was never accepted.

When gold was discovered in Australia that fall the hectic days of Forty-nine were repeated, and the *Nightingale* in spite of being a perfect lady joined the Rush. In fact she was the first to get away, sailing from Boston on October 18th. She took ninety days for this first passage to Melbourne but her later runs made up for it, nearly all being fast.

Sold in 1860, she fell into evil ways — and became a slaver. It wasn't her doing; she was helpless in the power of the notorious Prince of Slavers, Captain Francis Bowen, to be finally rescued by the U. S. sloop-of-war *Saratoga*. Her cargo of 961 slaves were set free at Monrovia and she was taken into the Federal service. Armed to the teeth, she joined the Gulf Blockading Squadron, and also served as supply and coal ship.

At the close of the War, under a number of owners, she sailed in the California and China trade. In 1876 she was sold to Norwegian interests and re-rigged as a bark for the American lumber trade. In 1893, forty-two years old, on a voyage from Liverpool to Halifax, she was abandoned at sea and foundered.

☆   ☆   ☆

The *Wild Wave* was a medium clipper, built in 1853 by

G. H. Ferrin of Richmond on the Kennebec. As fine a ship as ever came down the river and faster than most, in 1856 she made the passage from Callao to Plymouth in seventy days, a record that was never beaten. But it was her wrecking two years later, and the extraordinary pluck and ingenuity of her master that made the story of the *Wild Wave* a classic of the sea, and one that will live wherever a chart is unrolled.

Captain Josiah N. Knowles of Eastham, one of the best known Cape Cod shipmasters, was in command as the *Wave* cleared from San Francisco in 1858, bound for Valparaiso. She had a crew of thirty, ten passengers and two brass-bound chests containing eighteen thousand dollars in gold coin.

South Seas charts were not accurate in those days, and it is evident that the ship was far off her course, for in plotting it her officers assumed that the nearest land was twenty miles away. Instead, at one in the morning of March 5th, the lookout to his horror saw breakers directly under her lee bow. His warning shout to the quarterdeck brought instant action, but in attempting to come about the ship missed stays, and wearing, struck an uncharted reef.

In the turmoil of breakers and confusion, hardly five minutes passed before she lost her masts, bilged and rolled broadside to the raging seas. The breakers were so violent that the power of them tore the copper sheathing from the sides and bottom and tossed it up on deck.

It was impossible to launch boats, so the ship's people lashed themselves to whatever was handy and waited out the night. The passengers held up well, without panicking, the women with unexpected courage. At daybreak it was found the *Wave* had gone onto a circular reef, about two miles from a tiny coral atoll named Oeno, little more than a strip of sand half a mile wide.

The crew and passengers managed to get ashore with what livestock was aboard, and the bulk of the provisions. Shelters were built of driftwood and the sails of the ship. A well was dug in the sand, and proved to bring in fresh water. To add to the regular stores were an abundance of sea birds and their eggs, so the company was not depressed. If they had to be shipwrecked, it couldn't have been under better circumstances.

A few, however, couldn't help wondering about tidal waves — the atoll was barely a foot above sea-level.

After a week of preparation, the captain, the mate and five men put to sea in one of the boats that hadn't been stove in. They would attempt to reach the settlement of the *Bounty* mutineers on Pitcairn Island. They took the two chests of treasure with them. The parting from the rest of the company was not too happy, for their destination lay eighty miles to the south and those left behind doubted if they would make it.

It was a hazardous voyage that took three days. Due to the heavy surf they could not land in the Bay, but did get ashore on another part of the island, their boat stove beyond repair. The two chests were saved and buried ashore, but the party was disappointed to find the island uninhabited; the entire community had moved to Norfolk Island, they found out later. There was no worry for food; gardens were still growing, fruit trees laden and chicken, sheep and goats had been left behind. They could have lived on the island for the rest of their lives, and lived well, but they were not inclined toward the easy way of the mutineers. And the people of the *Wave* were depending upon them.

Yet to escape a boat was necessary, and a boat had to be built. Some discarded axes and other tools were found, and the party set to work. A schooner was what they intended, and they fashioned one, thirty feet long with an eight foot beam. Her construction was the result of much labor and ingenuity. They had no nails; to get some, the abandoned dwellings were burned. The nails salvaged were not enough, so wooden pegs were also used. A rusty anvil served as anchor, a copper kettle was the vessel's stove. Old rope was reduced to oakum and respun on an improvised wheel. Other gear was scraped together and canvas patched for sails.

They named the schooner *John Adams,* loaded the chests aboard and cast off, then set a course for Tahiti. Head winds that increased to gale force changed the destination to the Marquesas. For eleven days they rode out the storms, tossing like a chip on the mounting waves.

Three men had stayed on the island and the four aboard the little schooner dared not land at Resolution Bay on account of hostile natives, but pushed on to Muka Hiva where they were overjoyed to find the U. S. S. *Vandalia.*

They sold the schooner to a missionary for $250, and the Navy craft picked up the party left on Oeno and the three men on Pitcairn, carrying them all to Tahiti.

The people left on Oeno had spent their time in boatbuilding, too, constructing a whale boat from the wreckage of the *Wild Wave.* It was too well built; so heavy they could not get it in the water.

For all this setback their spirits had remained high and of the party of forty only one had died.

☆   ☆   ☆

According to the reports, "on good authority" the *Snow Squall* cost thirty thousand dollars to build, considered a substantial sum of money then. It was not necessary to seek buyers, for she was purchased off the stocks by Charles H. Green and Company of New York, and they made a sound investment. Fast and sturdy, she held a leading place among the small clippers for thirteen years. And even when twelve years old she showed a clean pair of heels to the Confederate cruiser *Tuscaloosa.*

The *Snow Squall* was a lively little ship, always ready for fun and frolic, and one wonders what her career might have been under a "canvas carrier"; a Searsport Pendleton for instance.

Instead, she spent her life in the China tea trade under command of Captain Ira Bursley, who knew how to get the best out of ship without being a driver.

Under his command she made a record voyage from New York to Melbourne in seventy-nine days. In 1856 she took a fling at the coffee trade and made the passage from New York to Rio in twenty-eight days, returning in thirty-four making a round trip that equaled any ever made.

Snow Squall was like a frisky mare champing at the bit. It was three years later that she took on one of Donald McKay's big clippers, the *Romance of the Sea. Romance* had the advantage of a thousand tons over the *Squall,* with a sail plan to match, but in a close race over the China course the little Maine ship beat her by two days to Sandy Hook. Alfred Butler of

South Portland could be proud of his creation, as were all the people of the Casco Bay region.

Kittery's *Typhoon* was launched fully rigged, with skysail yards aloft and colors flying, in February of 1851. A lot was expected of this ship with the sharp lines of a true clipper, and she more than came up to expectations. Owned by D. and A. Kingsland of New York, under command of Captain Charles H. Salter she made the passage from Portsmouth to Liverpool in the bad month of March in thirteen days and ten hours from wharf to dock. A feat unequaled up to this time, her maiden voyage earned her the title, and justly, of the "Portsmouth Flyer." Not only was she the first American clipper in the Mersey, she was also the largest merchant ship to be seen in Liverpool and was the sensation of the year.

After she returned to this country, the *Typhoon* sailed again in August in a race for California with two other ships, the *Raven* and *Sea Witch*. It was a classic of its kind; first one was ahead, then the other, and sometimes they sailed together over a long course.

A hard-fought passage, tack for tack, it was won by the *Raven,* 105 days from Boston to San Francisco compared to the *Typhoon's* 106. It was probably the only time she was beaten. She later made the passage from Calcutta to the Cape of Good Hope in thirty-seven days, a record that was equaled only once by the *Witch of the Wave,* built the same year as the *Typhoon,* at Portsmouth.

The financial panic of 1857 was the beginning of the end for the clipper ship era. Many Maine yards closed down, never to reopen.

The *Pocahontas,* built by the Houghtons of Bath, had the unique distinction of being the "last of the clippers" as well as the first of the Down Easters, and it is true that she had the best qualities of both. Launched in 1855, she was also said to have been the largest ship built up to that time. Classified as a "half-clipper" by Lloyd's, she made a record for cargo carrying as well as speed.

The coming of the Civil War in 1861 apparently gave the *coup de grace* to Maine shipping and shipbuilding, for on the Kennebec, the center of this activity then as it is today, a mere eleven vessels were built that year. Of these, seven were small coasters and sloops.

Chapter Eight

REBEL RAIDERS AND BLOCKADE RUNNERS

IN THE FIRST six months of the Civil War the northern shipping interests took a terrific beating from the activities of the Confederate raiders, which comprised both official naval cruisers and privateers. Nine fine large ships were lost from Bath alone and a total of ninety Maine vessels were taken in all, a frightful blow to the economy.

Sumter fell April 13, 1861. By May 29th nineteen northern vessels lay in the port of New Orleans as Confederate prizes — six of them from the State of Maine. Yet the losses Maine suffered were actually a blessing in disguise, for the resulting situation was instrumental in reviving the by then tottering shipbuilding industry.

It all came about by way of the "Alabama claims" against Great Britain, claims that were reminiscent of the French Spoliation Claims, with the difference that the Alabama claims were paid.

English neutrality had been proclaimed at the opening of the Rebellion, but England was far from neutral. This was indicated early in the war but especially pointed up by the "Alabama incident." In May of 1862 American agents discovered that a mystery ship was building at Lairds, designated only as No. 290. She was obviously intended as a man-of-war and just as obviously not for the Royal Navy. For whom, then, was she intended? It wasn't too difficult to guess, and Charles Francis Adams, the American minister, warned the British authorities that No. 290 was a Confederate cruiser, intended to operate in warfare against the United States. He asked that she be detained.

Her Majesty's Government demanded proof of this charge, which Adams promptly and amply supplied. The authorities then began a series of delaying tactics before their legal staff came up with the opinion that the mystery vessel should be detained. By that time the Confederate States of America cruiser

Alabama was already at sea.   Her crewmen were nearly all British subjects and at the Azores she received her armament and stores from two British ships, further proof if any were needed that the Government had known of the matter all along and were engaged actively in the intrigue.   Within a short time of being put in commission by Captain Raphael Semmes of the Confederate Navy, the Alabama had captured 12 vessels of the whaling fleet off Fayal.

By October the *Alabama* was on the Newfoundland Banks, in two weeks taking sixteen prizes.   The first Mainer to be taken was the bark *Lamplighter* of Calais, burned on the 15th.   With her cargo of tobacco she represented a loss of $117,600.   The next was the ship *Lafayette* from the Soule yard in Freeport, her cargo grain.   Five days later the bark *Loretta* of Damariscotta fell into the eager Rebel hands and was burned.   Next to be taken was the *Baron de Castine* of Castine.   And so it went: the *Washington* of Pittston, *Bethia Thayer* of Thomaston, *John A. Parks* of Hallowell, the *Louisa Hatch* of Rockland, the *Dorcas Prince* of Yarmouth, and the *Sea Lark* of Trescott whose value was estimated at $550,000.   She was followed by the *Jabez Snow* of Bucksport, the *Talisman* of Damariscotta, a Maine clipper; the *Anna T. Schmitt*, and the *Martha Wenzel* which was released through a maritime technicality.   Next the ship *Emma Jane* of Bath was burned and her crew put ashore at a small Indian Ocean town a considerable distance from their native soil of Maine.

Semmes and his *Alabama* had been having a high old time, but although they had no hint of it Fate in the form of a Mainer was about to lower the boom.

On June 11, 1864, the *Alabama* entered the port of Cherbourg, France, for refitting and to take on stores.   The United States cruiser *Kearsarge* was in the nearby port of Flushing.   And when word came that the hated enemy was close to hand the Mainer, for the *Kearsarge* had been built at Kittery Naval Yard, steamed post-haste to intercept.   She stood off Cherbourg and sent in a challenge to the Rebel to come out and fight.

The *Alabama* didn't like the look of the strutting *Kearsarge* with her bristling guns, but as a proud Southerner she was bound to accept and did, casting off and steaming out to meet the Yankee.

The French, meanwhile, not wishing to pass up any prospect of commerce or pleasure, ran special trains down from Paris so that by the time of the engagement all the shoreside vantage points were crowded by excited spectators.

The watchers got their money's worth, for the battle between the two Americans was a knock-down-and-drag-out affair. The righteous fury of the Maine-built craft could not be denied, and on that Sunday, June 21, 1864, the *Alabama's* career of destruction came to a violent end under the guns of the Federal cruiser.

☆   ☆   ☆

Other Confederate cruisers took their toll of Northern shipping: the *Tallahassee*, the *Chickamauga*, the *Georgia*, *Shenandoah* and *Florida* to name but a few. The *Tallahassee*, a captured blockade runner refitted as a cruiser, took seventeen Maine vessels alone.

The *Shenandoah* however, when she took the Maine bark *Delphine*, caught a Tartar.

She came aboard the Rebel cruiser by way of a bosun's chair and a yardarm whip, a caged canary in her hand and indignant fury in her heart. The wife of the captured bark's master, Captain William G. Nichols of Searsport, Mrs. Nichols wasn't one to stand any nonsense from a crew of Rebels. After directing the transfer of herself, her six-year old son, the steward's wife and all their gear from *Delphine* in the middle of the Indian Ocean, she turned her attention to the Confederate commander and gave him a dressing down to make his ears curl.

"Young Man," she said severely. "You should be ashamed of yourself, going round and sinking ships and barks belonging to honest folk. What would your mother say?"

The startled enemy blushed and hung his head. "She knows," he mumbled, "that I'm serving the Cause."

"That's another thing," Mrs. Nichols flared. "How dare you fire on the United States flag? You should be arrested."

And that's more or less what did happen to this Rebel, Lieut. Charles W. Read, who in the spring of 1863 was sent north on a roving commission. After he and his crew had apparently successfully cut out the revenue cutter *Caleb Cushing* from Portland Harbor they were chased and captured. Lieut.

Read was taken as a prisoner of war to Fort Preble where he is reported to have become so friendly with his captor Mainers that he had little spirit left for fighting against the North when he was later released to the Confederacy in an exchange deal.

Evidently the British had expected a Confederate victory, had gambled on it and lost. At the end of the War the United States had an open and shut case. Our Minister, Charles Francis Adams pressed the issue and in an 1871 treaty the entire matter was submitted to arbitration.

An impartial international commission found that in the cases of the *Alabama, Florida* and *Shenandoah,* the Crown officials had been "lacking in diligence." An award of $15,500,000 was made to the United States as damages, and the Maine shipping industry, which had been the greatest sufferer, was compensated accordingly. It was as a gift from the gods to the Maine maritime economy.

The decade between the peak of the clipper era and the beginning of the Down Easter could, perhaps, be called the "Era of Trial and Error," for the years shortly before, during and after the Civil War were indeed that. If successful the speculators with an urge to make a fast buck became leaders of industry and in many cases multi-millionnaires; if unsuccessful the least that could happen would be for them to be considered *persona non grata* in the best circles.

The hero with whom we are now concerned tried hard — Godfrey, how hard — but he failed probably for two reasons. The first was that the tides of chance were against him and the second that his heart wasn't actually in the undertaking, for he was hampered by an overly active conscience. Yet despite his failure, which involved great financial loss, he never lost the entree to the best homes and he died respected as a sea captain of the old school who had sailed both the Blue Water and coaster trade.

Captain Manasseh Tallets was in truth a fine old gentleman and one always ready with a helping hand. As a small boy I listened to his sea stories by the hour. A short man but sturdy, with keen blue eyes and a neat, close-cut gray beard, he was every inch a captain and forever looked as if he had just stepped off the quarterdeck.

When the Rebels fired on Fort Sumter and Old Glory was hauled down, Captain Tallets was as outraged as any other Portland man and more than some. "Hanging is too good for the ungrateful miscreants," he would declare hotly to any who would listen. His own nephew, his sister's boy, was one of the first to join up, serving in the Second Maine when it saved the Union Army and the Union while acting as rear guard at Bull Run. When the boy had entrained with his outfit Manasseh had been at the depot to see him off with a package of goodies and a twenty dollar bill for the new soldier's eager hand.

Manasseh at this time was full owner of the handsome topsail schooner *Nancy*, a vessel to make any mariner envious. Tall-masted, with a sleek black hull and high, sharp bows, she was an exceptionally fast sailer, and quick to answer.

Had it been the old days, Manasseh very likely would have turned the *Nancy* into a privateer, for which she was well fitted, but the word was coming up that the Confederate cruisers were on the prowl, and privateers too, and he wasn't minded to lose his fine, big craft to them. So he kept sweet *Nancy* in port where he could gaze on her fondly as often as he wished. This was expensive business, and moreover, people were beginning to talk.

Finally Manasseh had enough. He signed on a crew and loaded *Nancy* with a cargo of salt for a destination listed in the manifest as the West Indies. But by this time Captain Tallets had an open mind, and if salt proved to be in demand at higher prices in South America — or other places, he wouldn't be bound by his clearance papers. So the *Nancy* left Portland sailing free and easy and several days out was boiling along before a brisk nor'wester.

Manasseh paced the poop with a sedate and measured step, hands clasped behind his back, pausing from time to time to read the compass card over the helmsman's shoulder or to cast a weather eye aloft to study the billowing canvas. From all appearances he had everything under control, was completely at ease and satisfied with his lot, but it wasn't so. Captain Tallets had a problem that was growing bigger by the minute.

He put it from him as the mate came up the ladder and through the break. Punctual as usual, the officer paused to read the card, glanced aloft and reported to Manasseh.

"Course southeast by south," the master told him. "Hold her steady as she goes. The watch is yours, Mister Beal."

"Aye, aye, sir. Steady as she goes."

Manasseh nodded, went through the break and down the ladder to the companionway. In his own cabin he slumped into the big chair bolted to the deck behind the big table, also bolted. He leaned over the weighted-down open chart on the polished mahogany surface, studied the course as marked. He sighed and leaned back in the chair, knuckles of his hands white as they tightened on the arms. He stared at the tell-tale compass overhead, cast a glance at the chronometer and listened to the rush of water along the sides.

"She's fast, mortal fast," he mused. "She's doing all of nine knots and I'm not pushing her. My sweet *Nancy* is racing straight toward Opportunity. Seems a shame, sort of, to alter course - - -" He shook his head as if to clear it for better thinking, but his thoughts were disjointed and wild, for him. "She's fast, but is she fast enough to run the Blockade?"

There it was, out in the open. He recoiled in horror from the thought. Where was his patriotism? His beloved nephew, fighting for the Union, was perhaps at this very moment on some distant battlefield lying with a Minie ball in his heart.

Manasseh removed his outer garments and rolled onto his bunk. Sleep was a long time coming. The wash of the water, the creak of straining timbers all seemed to murmur, "Opportunity, Manasseh, opportunity. 1862 could be your big year. Salt, worth hardly more to the Cubans than at home is worth a fortune in the Confederacy — and you have a whole cargo aboard."

It was off the Virginia Capes that the *Nancy* first sighted the blockading fleet. The lookout called back, "Steamer bearing down two points off the starboard quarter!"

Manasseh on the poop focused his glasses. Like all loyal Union men he was interested in the rapidly growing force that gave promise of winning the war against the South.

Smoke pouring from her funnel, paddle wheels beating like threshing machines, walking beam working like a pump handle on a Portland handtub the Federal gunboat bore down. Signal flags fluttered from her gaff to "Heave-to!"

"Down helm," Manasseh ordered, and the *Nancy* headed into the wind, canvas slatting. As the gunboat came abreast he stared with considerable distaste at the pivot gun on the forward deck that swung to cover the schooner with a lethal eye.

A boat was lowered smartly and within minutes a young ensign came over the rail followed by an armed boarding party. The boy gave Manasseh a polite but stern salute. "Ensign Porter, sir. U. S. S. *Donelson*. May I inspect your papers, sir?"

"Have I any choice?" Manasseh grumbled.

The youngster grinned tightly. "No, sir."

The Portland captain led the way to his cabin, got out the papers and put them on the table. The ensign examined them carefully. "Everything is in order, sir. You may proceed."

The boarding party returned to the gunboat and the schooner resumed her course, her crew lining the rail and inspecting the blockading fleet with interest. Frigates, sloops-of-war, paddle wheel commercial steamers refitted and armed as gunboats, full-rigged ships, schooners; in fact, anything that would float.

"A fast craft, once it slipped between the blockading lines, could show a clean pair of heels to those scows." Manasseh stirred uneasily as the thought stayed with him. He felt a growing resentment that a Maine vessel flying the Stars and Stripes should have been boarded, while conceding that it had been done with the proper legal form. "I'm a mind to teach them a lesson," he muttered. "Daring to doubt my integrity."

"That's the talk," Fast Buck the tempter beamed. "You'll never find a better chance to get rich."

Before Manasseh could reply, Conscience took over. "It wouldn't be honest or patriotic," that wet blanket pointed out.

"I agree," Manasseh admitted faintly.

"Milksops, both of you," Fast Buck sneered.

"Even looking at it from your angle," Conscience demanded. "What about the blockading fleet?"

"The *Nancy* is faster than anything the Navy has."

The moon would be full that night, but when the sun set behind a bank of clouds Manasseh made up his mind. With the moon's face hidden by the growing scud he would run the Blockade. He would make a fortune.

To the surprise of the mates and crew, he ordered the *Nancy* to come about, to stand on and off until dark. The scud was now really heavy, the moon when it rose all but hidden, yet casting a dim light to navigate by. When the tide turned, he sent the schooner rushing through the Blockade line apparently undiscovered. The mates and crew, now informed, were as eager as he for their promised shares.

It was tricky business and Manasseh's first experience as a law-breaker, and he thanked his Maker for the sweet-sailing *Nancy*. "Once safely back in Portland, I'll donate money for a field hospital," he told Conscience.

"Manasseh, I'm ashamed of you," the reply came back sadly.

"That makes two of us," Manasseh agreed. He stared hard into the night. The schooner was doing twelve, maybe fourteen knots. Then he heard the terrifying sound of paddle wheels!

He had not considered the possibility that the Union fleet might have formed a second and inner line. At that very moment the moon came from behind the clouds, and it was bright as day. And there hardly a cable's length away off the port bow was the U. S. S. *Donelson*!

This time the gunboat didn't break out any signal bunting. Instead a shot was fired across *Nancy's* bows.

When young Ensign Porter came over the rail followed by the boarding party, Manasseh was amazed that a boy of his years could look so downright mean.

☆ ☆ ☆

Captain Tallets lived to a ripe old age, and he spent most of it in an effort to obtain compensation from the United States Government for the loss of his schooner and cargo. A small fortune was used up on lawyers and lawsuits, and his claims were finally carried to the Supreme Court — to no avail.

A fine old gentleman, and a fascinating spinner of deep-sea yarns, he always wound up his story-telling with some reference to the blockade-running fiasco. "Doesn't seem right that the Government should take a man's vessel and cargo," he would mutter, a perplexed frown wrinkling his brow.

Even a boy could see the fallacy of this thinking. "You were lucky they didn't send you to a place where you'd never hear the dogs bark," I said. "You must admit the *Nancy* was taken where no honest Union schooner had a right to be."

Captain Tallets had an answer for that one. "Any seaman knows that the wind and tide can trouble the best navigator. Furthermore, the cross-currents are almighty treacherous along that coast. What if the *Nancy* was off a bit from her chartered course? Should I, as master and owner, be penalized for an act of God?"

Chapter Nine

QUITE BY ACCIDENT

IN 1850 THE Lincolnville-built bark *Georgiana,* Captain Rufus Benson, hailing from Camden, Maine, cleared from that Penobscot Bay port with a cargo of lime, destination New Orleans. Both Captain Benson and his mate Joseph Graffam were Camden men, as was Robert J. Burd, twenty-one, a member of the five-man crew.

After a slow, uneventful voyage, the bark arrived at New Orleans and discharged her cargo. Before she could laden for return, the bark was chartered by unnamed parties through a shipping agent. Captain Benson was mildly disturbed over this, yet such procedure was not unknown when the agent was a man of integrity. Although this one had dealt with the owners for some years, Captain Benson wanted more information.

"You haven't a thing to worry about," the agent explained. "Your bark is simply chartered to take a large number of workmen to the mines in Chagras, in South America."

"Then why the secrecy?"

"It's plain to see that you are not familiar with the Big Business methods," the agent allowed smugly. "No offense meant, but your innocence in this respect is quite obvious."

"Maybe it is, and maybe it isn't. Answer my question."

The agent nodded. "Labor is hard to get, especially trained miners. The American mine operators are in labor competition with the British, French and German interests. If it were known that my principals were shipping a bark-load of miners, opposition agents would immediately swarm around with better offers."

Captain Benson was satisfied, if a trifle dubious. He took on stores and replaced worn gear, and by sailing time everything aboard was shipshape and Bristol fashion. Only trouble was, the walking cargo hadn't showed and he was due to cast off within the hour. He paced the deck nervously.

Shortly before the tide turned, a mob of noisy ruffians made their appearance, herded down the dock by crimps and bully boys armed with clubs, blackjacks and knuckle dusters. They seemed to be of every nationality, as well as the dregs of the waterfront. Nearly all were staggering drunk, the few sober ones with the look of wretches who would cut their mother's throat for the price of a drink. Staggering or not, they were able to fight, and in the process of embarkation one of the warriors had his head bashed in.

"What are you going to do about him?" the Maine captain asked, pointing to the still twitching corpse.

"That's easy." The chief crimp grabbed the body by the ankles and rolled it into the harbor.

Before Captain Benson could report the incident to the authorities, the bully boys assumed complete charge of the bark as well as of the unruly "workmen." The mooring lines were cut, a tug came alongside, made fast and towed the bark to midstream and the river's mouth. Then the tug cast off. The shocked bark from Camden was on her own.

Captain Benson stared at Mate Graffam. "So this is Big Business, and these cutthroats miners?" He realized that he'd been taken, and he wondered what the owners would say. "It's a mess, for fair."

The leader of the bully boys, a red-haired, hard-faced type, swaggered over. "What's the trouble, mister?"

"Captain," the Mainer said sternly.

"Captain," the hoodlum repeated genially. "What I want to know, is anything wrong?"

"Nothing that can't be adjusted, given time," Benson replied grimly.

The chief thug returned to the quarterdeck. With a grin, he drew a huge Navy revolver. He was a very tough character, he told the Mainers, and he'd just as soon use the weapon as not. However, in the interests of efficiency and proper navigation he would rather hold his fire. It was up to them to call the turn.

"In that case," the Maine captain said, "Hold your fire."

"Fine," the pleased pirate beamed. "Set a course for Chagras, as the charter calls for."

Benson gave the necessary orders. "I'd like to know about one thing: how you expect this waterfront scum to do any mining? I doubt if they ever handled a pick and shovel in their misspent lives, let alone a drill."

"They'll be whipped into shape when they sober up," the friendly thug replied. "As for being miners, actually they're underminers." He winked, headed for the break, dropped down the ladder for the waist, evidently bound for a tour of inspection.

Benson was still simmering at the takeover of his vessel when it made Woman's Island at the mouth of the Yucatan and dropped her hook. Legally, he could hardly complain for it had been chartered, even if the methods used by his passengers were not exactly orthodox. To ease his fury was thought of the charter money, already paid to the agent. He hoped the owners hadn't let the insurance lapse.

Presently a handsome brig, the *Susan Loud* of Boston, Captain Simeon Pendleton, made in to the anchorage. Simeon was an old friend and former Camden man. His mate was Thomas Hale.

It was nice to meet up with home folks in this misbegotten end of nowhere. Benson felt better, somewhat, when he learned that the brig, too, was crammed to the brim and running over with "miners."

Next day a steamer rounded the Island; a tramp from the United States. Word got out that she was loaded with arms and ammunition. Captain Benson saw the light. A revolution, by thunder! And he and his crew were right smack in the middle of it! "We're neutrals," he told the mate. "We'll stay neutral."

The steamer, along with her lethal cargo, carried an important passenger, none other than the famous Cuban revolutionist General Narcisco Lopez. For some time the better-class Cubans had been restive under Spanish rule. They wanted independence and now they intended to do something about it. They organized an underground movement and stated publicly that they would join any force invading the island for the purpose of overthrowing its Spanish government.

Lopez and others had organized such a force in New Orleans. The so-called miners were hired mercenaries, with a scattering of Cuban patriots among them. Now they were all transferred to the steamer and Captain Pendleton of the *Loud* was taken along as pilot. The expedition arrived at Cardenas May 19th and formed a beachhead, but the local underground didn't rise as promised and the defense proved hot and getting hotter. The patriot "army" reembarked and with smoke pouring from her funnel the steamer raced for Florida, a Spanish cruiser in close pursuit.

By burning everything combustible aboard the steamer made her escape. General Lopez promptly began organizing a new expedition, and Captain Pendleton left for home. The two vessels, with their remaining officers and men, had stayed behind and were lying at the mouth of the Yucatan blissfully unaware of what was in store when a Spanish man-of-war, trailed by an armed brig, suddenly rounded the island and trained its guns on the Yankee craft. Both were towed to Havana, the seamen held captive for many months, interrogated frequently and allowed just enough food to keep them alive. Finally, through the efforts of the United States Government and Americans living in Cuba, they were released.

The officers of the two captured vessels did not fare so well. Captain Benson and Mate Graffam of the *Georgiana*, and Mate Thomas Hale of the *Susan Loud*, were tossed into a dungeon deep down in Morro Castle, heavily ironed and chained to a damp stone wall, where they could listen to the waves lapping against the outside. After nearly a year of this they were brought to trial and found guilty, condemned to the chain gang for life, and carried to Spain to begin their sentence.

When Sarah Graffam, mother of the mate, heard the news, instead of panicking she set to work to obtain the prisoners' release. She left Camden for Washington and aroused the country on the way by means of the press and addresses to various organizations. In the capital she put pressure on the Maine men in Congress and gained interviews with the President and Secretary of State. Not satisfied with all this, she took passage for Cuba where she made life miserable for the Spanish officials. She was readying for the journey to Spain to take the matter up personally with the King and Queen when word came that,

at the request of the United States Government, the prisoners
had been released and were on their way home.

The bark and brig were never recovered, but the American
officers were safe. That was what counted. Once the joyful
reunion with her son was over, Mrs. Graffam wrote a letter of
thankful appreciation to the "public of the United States" for
its powerful assistance.

☆   ☆   ☆

In 1860 the Thomaston ship *Frank Flint*, 1193 tons, Captain Ed Robinson, was in Liverpool. England was having
trouble with China over the opium trade, a very profitable one
to the British merchants. The Chinese Government wanted the
importation of the drug from India stopped. It was demoralizing the Chinese people they said, and it was, not only by use of
the drug itself but by graft in high places. Whether the British
liked it or not the trade was going to be stopped. So the Government cracked down on the importers, who immediately resorted
to smuggling which was even more profitable, although large
sums had to be paid to conniving Chinese officials.

Something drastic had to be done. The merchants were
putting pressure on Her Majesty's Government, and the "City,"
London's financial district, was taking a very dim view of the
whole affair. There was but one way to resolve the problem —
a good war with China.

Events in India indirectly furnished the excuse. Native
British troops had been issued muzzle-loader cartridges wrapped
in oiled paper. To load a musket it was necessary to bite the
top off the cartridge. When sly agents of a foreign power
pointed out to the Hindus that the oil was from the fat of a
cow, an animal sacred to them, all hell broke loose. When the
same agents explained to the fanatical Moslems that the oil on
the cartridge paper came from a pig and to touch their lips to
it was an act of pollution, as any True Believer was quite aware,
the Followers of the Prophet were aghast.

Although the two schools of religious thought were opposed,
the reactions of all the native soldiers were identical, and the
Great Mutiny was the result.

England rushed troops to India, and there was considerable
unpleasantness all round. And while the British were busy trying to bring back the status quo there the Chinese Government

decided to take advantage of the heaven-sent opportunity to officially put an end to the opium trade. They seized an English smuggling vessel and placed the master and his crew in a very untidy dungeon.

But although seemingly shocked by this treachery the British were really far from displeased. The British governor at Hong Kong was able to order the bombardment of Canton, thus launching a war for which China, after ten years of civil conflict known as the Taiping Rebellion, was in no way prepared.

H. M. S. *Odin* was ordered to the Far East to assist General Gordon in his punitive measures, and every vessel in the British home ports was commandeered as a troopship to send out reinforcements. Among the vessels commandeered at Liverpool was the Yankee *Frank Flint*. When her Captain, Ed Robinson, was informed that both he and his ship were now in Her Majesty's Service he didn't like it, not one bit, but he was trapped and knew it. He took on a cargo of cavalrymen and their mounts, and required provisions, mostly livestock comprising ducks and hens but in addition including a few cows which were quartered between decks with the horses, so that feeding time sounded like daybreak down on the farm.

It was a long voyage round the Cape of Good Hope, across the Indian Ocean, through the Java Straits, and up the China Seas to Tientsin. On arrival, the troops were quickly disembarked, formed up and sent off on the double to the front lines where Gordon and Lord John Hay were teaching the enemy respect for the Union Jack. The young wife of the *Flint's* master expressed a wish to view the coming battle, and she was promptly strapped into an armchair and hoisted to the yardarm where it was made fast. Here, somewhat exposed, she got the thrill of her twenty-two years.

The battle was of short duration, for the Chinese, armed with swords and bow-guns, were no match for the highly trained and well-equipped professional soldiers of the "foreign devils."

As soon as the fighting stopped the ladies from the many vessels in the harbor insisted on going ashore. They wanted to see if Tientsin lived up to the meaning of its name, "Heaven's Ford." So they were all gathered in one party, including the

eager Mrs. Robinson, and on horseback under armed escort rode
into the city while the battle smoke still hung heavy over the
land and awkwardly sprawled bundles of dirty, blood-soaked
rags still littered the highway.

The ladies, in a well-bred effort not to embarrass their escort, averted their genteel gaze as the horses daintily stepped
over the obstructions. They couldn't help but hear the comment
of one officer "that the natives got what they bloody well de-
served for daring to defy Europeans."

All in all it was a pleasant excursion, and some of the ladies
voiced a regret that a picnic lunch had not been brought along.

Finally, as it was getting on toward tea time, the party
returned to the waterfront. After thanking the escort, the
ladies were helped into the waiting boats and returned to their
various ships.

"Well, my dear," Captain Ed said, as his young wife came
over the side. "Did you enjoy yourself?"

"Immensely. It was all so strange. Of course, there were
a lot of dead people around, but we just ignored them. The poor
things are probably better off, under the circumstances." She
turned large eyes on the Captain. "What will the authorities
do now. The French and British, I mean?"

"Likely strike out for Peking," Captain Ed said thoughtfully. "Tientsin is only the port for the capital. It didn't make
much of a defense. Couldn't, with only a walled section of three
miles. I misdoubt if Peking will be so easy to take."

"Are we going along?" his lady asked breathlessly.

Peking would be a harder nut to crack, for it was a great
city of walls within walls, covering an area of twenty-five
square miles, with plenty of troops for defense. Within the
city was the "Imperial City," and in the center of the "Imperial
City" was the "Forbidden City." This last named "City" was
surrounded by massive pink walls and a moat, and here were
the royal palaces.

The Emperor, Hien Fung, with his Empress, Tze Hai,
should have felt reasonably secure for by Chinese standards
Peking was well fortified. Evidently they had little faith in
their army or the willingness of the panicked inhabitants to

stand in defense, so they lit out for the hinterlands, an example that was quickly followed by the entire population.

When the attacking columns entered the gates it was to discover a city of the dead. The Grand High Palace, the "Hall of Highest Peace" was deserted except for two tiny Pekingese dogs, pets of the Empress, who barked defiantly at the invaders. With that courage for which they are known, they tried to defend the possessions of their mistress, but the palace was completely looted and the dogs themselves taken by the expedition commander, Sir John Hay. They had the distinction of being the first Pekingese in England.

Captain Ed, with other shipmasters, had gone in with the troops after sternly refusing the plea of his wife to accompany him. So the lady sulked aboard the *Flint* and the Captain went along to share in the spoils. The Mainer did all right for himself and Mrs. Ed was completely mollified when she beheld the large collection of "curios" with which he returned.

The list is long: an inlaid rose cabinet (1,500 pieces of inlay), a nest of four lacquer tea tables, two sets of lacquer trays (one in dark red, the other in gold) a tea caddy with gold dragon's feet, a sewing box, a gold lacquer writing desk, a box for gloves, a tiny chess table, boxes of ebony, sandlewood and ivory, a carved ivory brooch, a carved ivory basket, a steel mirror in a case, hand-carved bamboo vases, a lacquer opium dish — and many smaller items.

The most valuable items were a gold lacquer table, three feet in diameter, its pedestal surmounted by dragon's feet (now in the Knox Memorial at Thomaston), and richly embroidered robes with gold buttons that had been worn by the Emperor and Empress.

Captain Robinson also took into protective custody bolts of fine silks, from the warehouse at Tientsin. He presented many to Mrs. Flint, wife of a partner in Chapman and Flint, co-owners with him of the *Frank Flint*. To her twelve year old son, he gave a Chinese bow-gun.

"I never did and still don't hold with looting," Captain Ed was apt to explain in later years. "But I was fearful that these rare objects of art would fall into unappreciative and vandal hands."

Mr. Merry, one-time second mate of the brig *Jasper*, like Captain Polite of the Pacific Coast and a later day, lived up to his name. For Mr. Merry was a merry soul indeed, able to see humor in everything, and his big booming laugh was forever sounding over the vessel to the annoyance of her company from the Captain on down to Doc's mate. It seemed like the dastard never slept.

Even when a foremast hand displeased him, and it was often, Mr. Merry would smile, a trifle wolfishly it is true, while he pointed out to the offender the error of his ways. And when he "blew the man down" with a belaying pin, kicked him into the scuppers and stomped him into insensibility the second mate would laugh uproariously in full enjoyment of his good, clean fun.

It got so whenever the foremast hands heard his wholesome, unrestrained laughter they would shiver in their boots, and the captain in his cabin would stiffen over the chart and brace himself for the screams that were sure to follow. That Mister Merry was a Bucko Mate is evident, yet he was a Bucko long before his time. In the early years of the century they had not evolved. They came in with the clippers, when the crews were becoming Outlander or foreigner-ridden. An all-Maine crew would not stand for such treatment.

Mister Merry was five foot nine, well set up, with fists that were lethal weapons. Under a mop of sandy hair his merry blue eyes twinkled out of a round, apple-cheeked face. Like so many of the latter-day Buckos he never used profanity or drank, and shoreside he spent his time in church, or discoursing learnedly with literary groups. He once said he hailed from Jonesport, a statement no one bothered to check.

Time passed. Crews wouldn't sign on for a second voyage. The captain and mate knew why and decided that something must be done, and fast. They must get rid of Mister Merry, a chore not easy for he was a first-rate officer, an expert sailor, and the owners took him at his smiling face value. Then the mate had an idea. "Slade is looking for a mate. It would be a step up for Mister Merry. He'd likely jump at it."

The Old Man was doubtful. "Slade is a slaver," he pointed out. "Mister Merry would never sign on as mate aboard a Middle Passage ship." Slade was not only a slaver, he was the King of Slavers, and infamous for his brutality to the cargo.

The mate thought on it. "Slade is a smooth talker. I'll get him to tell Merry he has reformed, but needs a good man as mate to keep him on the straight and narrow. Once he's aboard the *Warrior Prince* and at sea, it will be too late."

"Mister Merry won't take kindly to being hornswoggled," the captain said.

"What do we care? We'll be well rid of him. Slade will be the target for his ire. A character like Slade deserves what he gets."

The captain was still dubious. "A scheme like this one usually backfires."

Despite the Old Man's anxiety the scheme was put forward and it worked out according to plan. That is, they got rid of Mister Merry. But knowing Mister Merry, the captain was almost sorry for the slaver and his near-pirate crew. Likely by the end of the voyage they would all be carrying prayer books — along with their bumps and bruises.

☆   ☆   ☆

Some ships were money-makers, and some ships got by, like humans who try hard and find the going difficult. The seven-hundred-ton Yarmouth-built ship *Helios*, Captain Benjamin Webster, was a money-maker. Nor was her money-making a flash in the pan; she kept right on harvesting the interesting stuff for all her days.

It was not long after the fall of Fort Sumter that *Helios* cleared Baltimore laden with copper ore, carefully feeling her way out of Chesapeake Bay where all aids to navigation had been removed by the Rebels. She made Liverpool in nineteen days, sold the ore on a high market and took on a cargo of salt for Wyborg, Finland, where she took on deals (heavy timbers) for Bordeaux. Here she was chartered for San Francisco, at the pleasant sum of fifteen thousand dollars in gold. Gold was then at a premium, so *Helios* netted thirty thousand which was even more pleasant.

In San Francisco she took on a cargo of wheat, flour and oats for Melbourne and made the passage in forty-two days. In Melbourne a pack of chattering Chinese were taken aboard at fifteen dollars per head. To accommodate them, berths were set up between decks and a galley built on deck.

That wasn't all she took on at Melbourne. She signed on "Chinese" Boggs!

"Why are you called 'Chinese?' the Captain asked suspiciously, when Boggs applied for third mate's berth, then vacant.

"Because of my unusual fluency in the Chinese dialects, sir," Boggs replied smoothly.

As already stated, the Maine ship was loaded with the yellow men, and not one officer or crew member knew the lingo. The future had looked grim indeed. Now, like the answer to a shipmaster's prayer, Boggs showed up.

"Let's hear you spout some." The Captain settled back in his chair, like a modern TV producer giving an audition.

Boggs knew exactly four words of Cantonese and quite a bit of pidgen English, and that was it. He needed the job. By giving his voice a high pitch and mixing in some double-talk, he managed to put on a fairly respectable show.

The Old Man was definitely impressed, as was the mate who had entered the cabin while Boggs was sounding off. A slow grin spread over his lean Maine face. "Captain, we are all set."

The Captain wasn't going to be rushed into anything. "Let me see your papers." He examined them carefully. "You seem to have been on the beach for some time."

"That's because I was waiting for the proper ship — this one, sir," the quick-thinking Boggs said. "Such a fine ship."

"It says here that your given name is Ivan. Are you part Russian?"

"No sir. Ivan is the Russian form of John. Actually, Ivan is an old English name. My folks were English."

"All right." The Old Man opened his book. "Sign here." The formalities over, he told his new third, "Mister Boggs, you will take full charge of the passengers. From now on they are your responsibility."

"Aye, aye, sir."

After his gear was stowed, Boggs marched bravely down to interview his charges. Ringed by fifty impassive Oriental faces, he asked, low-voiced, "Anybody here speak English?"

His only answer was complete silence and continued slant-eyed scrutiny. Reluctantly he added, "There's money in it. Much money."

A little man with a long pigtail, hands hidden in flowing sleeves, trotted forward and bowed. "English like a book, Cull," he said, in that difficult Market Street dialect. "If there's loot enough to make it worth while."

☆ ☆ ☆

The English-speaking passenger was named Ling Su, and he was willing to discreetly transmit orders from Boggs to the Chinese, for a substantial "consideration." This arrangement was so successful and the Captain so pleased to have an officer who spoke the outlandish lingo, after he delivered the Chinese at Hong Kong he took aboard another batch, bound States-side. To the concern of Mister Boggs, several had a smattering of English. When the Captain learned that fact, he was bound to learn that Boggs could not speak Chinese. Glumly Mister Boggs checked them up the gangplank.

"Don't worry about it, Cull," a voice soothed at his elbow. "I'll be right there to keep them under control."

"You were discharged at Hong Kong," the relieved third told Ling Su. "Anyway, how can a little cuss like you keep such a mob under control?"

"My cousin is in this group, a very important person, an enforcer for one of the tongs. In San Francisco we called such 'hatchet men.'"

"Will he cooperate?"

"For a consideration. And by the way, Boggs, I feel that it is only fair for me to get a cut of the bonus the Old Man paid you."

The cargo, walking and bulk, was discharged at San Francisco. Then followed another round trip to China, with a group returning to the Land of their Ancestors, and another bound for California. Ling and his cousin, the hatchet man, were now fixtures aboard, and Boggs had trouble keeping their continued presence from the sharp eyes of the mate. "Boggs," he said one day. "Two of those Chinks look almighty familiar. They seem to be aboard on every voyage."

"All Chinks look alike to western eyes," Boggs allowed. "Even to a Chinese expert like me."

"Yes, and You are doing all right for yourself," the mate agreed enviously. "The Old Man sets great store by you. How do you manage to take care of all your dough?"

"It's easy," Mister Boggs told him, and this was true enough, for he didn't see much of it. After the two Chinese cousins had their cut, they usually won the balance by way of fan tan.

Chapter Ten

SAIL CARRIERS AND CANVAS SPREADERS

IN THE DAYS of sail, Bowditch Cemetery at Searsport, Maine, the little Penobscot Bay town that boasted of more than a hundred sea captains, was said to contain more tombstones than coffins. This was a phenomenon not to be particularly wondered at for Searsport captains were all "Sail Carriers," and the inscription "Lost at Sea" was often carved on the monuments set up in memory of the dear departed.

A typical inscription reads: "In memory of Captain John G. Pendleton, son of Captain Phineas, Jr., and Wealthy C. Pendleton, born April 23, 1836, master of the ship *Solferino*, which was lost at sea with all on board, bound from Rangoon to London, last spoken off Cape of Good Hope, December 21, 1863."

An earlier John Pendleton had been lost at sea on December 2, 1847, when the schooner *Mary Brooks*, bound from Havana to Boston, foundered. There were no less than twenty-five Pendletons numbered among the Searsport shipmasters, and to relate the life story of any one of them, many shorter than they should have been, is likely to make the reader's blood run cold and hair stand on end — for the Pendletons were confirmed Sail Carriers.

In an era when a skipper would rather have a reputation for sail carrying than any other attribute of seamanship, Searsport was a leader in the dangerous art, and of the Searsport masters the Pendleton family stood out as experts.

Although a choice is difficult, perhaps young John G. Pendleton, master and owner of the *William H. Connor* might be considered the greatest "canvas spreader" and "kite flyer" of all the Pendletons. A big man with big ideas, young John claimed a ship had masts and yards, and canvas to bend on, so why not use it?

When he married Sarah Gilkey, comely daughter of another important Searsport family, he could think of no better way to spend a honeymoon than a voyage aboard the *Connor*. One day, outbound under a strong westerly, Sarah, somewhat weary of being tossed about the cabin, managed to work her way out of the companionway, up the ladder and through the break to the quarterdeck. Not a timid sort, and used to ships and the sea, she felt that as a young woman of common sense, and duty-minded, some mild remonstrance was in order. "John, dear," she said to her husband, "it's getting awfully trembly in the cabin. Wouldn't it be well to shorten sail?"

The man at the wheel stiffened, the mate paused in his pacing in dismay and the captain looked down at his bride with an amused smile. No one else aboard would have the courage to suggest such a thing — to him. Take in sail for a mild blow like this? Then the captain recollected that his wife was only a female. To save trouble later, it might be best to explain the whys and wherefores.

Before he could start, the main topgallant sail blew out of the bolt ropes and vanished downwind. "Well, my dear," Captain Pendleton remarked dryly, "there's one sail we don't need worry about."

Sarah looked aloft and then out over the roaring sea. "Yes," she said in a small voice. She went below, relieved somewhat, but still taxed by anxiety. And with reason. Before the watch was out another main topgallant had been bent and set.

☆ ☆ ☆

The sea is a backdrop for great traditions, and many are the Maine families whose sons went down to the sea to seek their fortunes, and incidentally, High Adventure. Yet it is doubtful if anywhere, at any time, a family of seafarers came up to the Searsport Pendletons.

Captain Phineas Pendleton, born at Stonington, Connecticut, September 26, 1780, was founder of the family in Maine. With his parents, Lt. Peleg and Ann Park Pendleton, he moved to Searsport, then called Prospect, by way of the sea; probably in the schooner *Dolphin* of which his father owned a portion and held command. Like all boys of that age young Phineas was eager to follow in the footsteps of his ancestors, to someday sail to distant lands as master of his own ship.

He did hold command, but only in the sloop *Alexander* in 1805, and the schooner *Belfast* in 1812, although it is possible there were other vessels unrecorded. His sons and grandsons, however, made up for this lack, for they held command in every type vessel that sailed from Yankeeland.

Perhaps Phineas surmised that he would never tread the quarterdeck of a full-rigged ship, and wanted anchors to the windward, or perhaps he was just downed by Cupid's darts. At any rate, he up and married this Searsport girl, Nancy Gilmore, and together they turned out a family of twelve, all of a pattern; the males becoming sea captains, the females marrying sea captains. These dutiful children followed in their parents footsteps, and the resulting line of Pendletons was one to be proud of. Being from the same pattern, although some were sharper of bows, or broader of beam, or rigged differently, they were fairly easy to recognize, whether in Hong Kong, San Francisco, or New York. Every Pendleton man who held command, held it well, and it must be confessed that they all had the same vice — Sail Carrying!

A Pendleton on the quarterdeck was like a racehorse at the barrier, eager and anxious to go. And once the tugs cast off and the pilot was dropped, on would go the canvas; not a stitch at a time, as needed, but every sail at once, and by Jupiter, those vessels would surely go.

It was said that while nearly every shipmaster navigated by Bowditch, Pendletons sailed by Pendleton. And such was the ability of these men that comparatively few were the mishaps despite swift passages. And in such an event, it was always a Pendleton who paid the piper. Another headstone would rise above an empty grave in Searsport cemetery, neatly inscribed, "Lost at Sea."

The record, an amazing one, speaks for itself. The list of vessels commanded by descendants of Phineas Pendleton I, reads like the history of the United States Merchant Marine, before steam came in. Think of it. Forty-one great tall-masted, full-rigged ships, all of famous names; thirty-three barks, twenty-seven schooners, fourteen brigs, one barkentine and one sloop. A grand total of one hundred seventeen vessels commanded in a single family!

Captain Curtis of the *Tillie E. Starbuck* was a noted Sail Carrier, and with the well-known Donald Nicholson as mate this vessel made some very fast passages. *Tillie*, though, couldn't hope to compete with the wooden ships of her time and class in speed.

It wasn't that *Tillie* didn't try hard. She was as willing a female as ever cut the waves; she was easy to handle, and a smart sailer. And just as Captain Curtis and his mate were Canvas Carriers, *Tillie* was a Canvas Spreader. Only trouble with *Tillie* was, she was made of iron. In fact, she was the first full-rigged ship ever built of iron in the United States. Launched April 14, 1883, from the yard of John Roach at Chester, Pennsylvania, she was a fine craft of 2033 tons, 257 feet in length, 270 feet overall.

The more conservative members of the shipping circles were inclined to doubt the capabilities of an iron sailing ship, and when it was learned that *Tillie*, where she wasn't iron was steel, they one and all "viewed with alarm." So much so that the underwriters were concerned, to the extent of raising the insurance rates.

As if to further annoy conservative Maine thought, *Tillie* had an all-steel bowsprit and three hollow masts made of the best fire-box steel, strengthened inside with angle iron. Her lower yards were ninety feet, the topsail yards on her fore and main were seventy-two feet. She had single topgallant yards and three standing skysail yards.

W. A. Rogers was her first master, a sound man and a fine navigator, but nothing fancy in the way of sail carrying. He handed over to Captain Curtis in the nineties, and immediately *Tillie* perked up, rolled her eyes and put on a new face, the years falling away as if by magic. When Don Nicholson, the fabulous mate came aboard, she could hardly wait to put to sea.

Captain Curtis and Don did well by her, and had she been a ship of wood the three of them would have broken every record on the Seven Seas. As it was, she made one fast passage after another, but the iron in her frame and plates held her back, strive as she might, and it finally got into her soul. She settled down then to a steady, rather humdrum existence, like a young matron when she realizes that the honeymoon is over. At the turn of the century, when Luckenback bought her, she was scared witless that she'd be converted into a barge, but Welch and Company saved her from that terrible fate. With San

Francisco as her home port, and Captain W. W. Winn in command, *Tillie* started life anew.

Bound out to Honolulu from New York in 1907, the *Tillie E. Starbuck* was lost off the Horn. The crew were rescued by a British vessel, but the mate went down with the great iron ship.

The *Alfred D. Snow* was built and owned by Old Sam Watts of Thomaston. A big 2075-ton ship, the black-hulled beauty was a fit subject for the brush of a marine artist, as in fact she often was. A fine ship and fast, she had one fault. She was very, very cranky, and would not stand up until she had exactly eight hundred tons of ballast in her.

This particular trait, together with a few others, and the belief that her master, Captain Willey, was a confirmed Sail Carrier, did not suggest the *Snow* as a haven of security for timid seamen, and one might assume, therefore, that she would have difficulty in signing on a crew. The contrary was true, and seamen were anxious to sail with the tall-masted ship, perhaps due to sporting instincts or a desire to live dangerously.

Captain Willey didn't give the impression of being a careless captain or the wildest of sail carriers; in fact, it is doubtful if he was, for he had always been a fine seaman and navigator, a master who knew his trade from A to Z.

As to his sail carrying proclivities, there were two schools of thought on that. Some old hands gave him a character for recklessness, while others claimed he was as cautious as an old maid who had inadvertently made her way into a waterfront dive. Nonetheless, the proof of the pudding was in the eating, as Sam Watts was fond of remarking, and what happened to the *Alfred D. Snow* spoke for itself.

As one oldtimer put it: "I was very well acquainted with Captain Willey of the *Alfred D. Snow*. . . . Captain Willey had but one ambition; that was to make a fast passage. He had a ship that could sail fast, and he knew it. He was only eighty days out when he piled her up on Dunmore Head."

The oldtimer continues, in his article for SEA BREEZES, an English magazine: "He was a very venturesome man. He was known to run seven days on dead reckoning without a sight . . . expected to end his days shipwrecked. He was picked up warm on the beach."

On the other hand, friends declared that he had never been known as a reckless sail carrier, nor did his appearance give that impression. A quiet man, about forty-five years of age, with black hair, mustache and side whiskers, he did impress folk with his air of calm assurance.

On her last voyage in 1888, the *Snow* loaded with general cargo from New York for San Francisco. At San Francisco, she took on wheat for Liverpool. Caught in a great gale that roared across the British Isles, the big square-rigger was driven onto the Irish coast with a loss of all hands.

An officer of the *Joseph B. Thomas*, another of Sam Watts' big ships, in Bristol at the time, crossed the Irish Sea to identify the bodies washed up on the beach. He was able to identify those of Captain Willey, John Lermond, the carpenter and several others, all Thomaston men.

☆　☆　☆

Of all the Searsport Pendleton family of shipmasters, Captain Phineas Pendleton III was probably the most famous. Not that he had more ability or courage than the others, but he commanded the *Henry B. Hyde* for her first eight voyages, then turned the command over to his son, Phineas Jr.

The *Henry B. Hyde* has always been considered the finest and fastest full-rigger built in the United States after the clipper era. A beautiful ship, she was launched at the Bath, Maine, yard of John McDonald in November of 1884. She made record passages and money for her owners, and while she was never a "hell-ship" or "blood-boat," she was a hard ship for foremast hands.

This was not due to brutality on the part of her officers, but to the stern discipline maintained, stemming possibly from the fact that the officers were all Yankees, and the crews generally Britishers who were apt to refer to her as "that damned Yankee hot-box, the *'Enery 'Ide*."

On February 24, 1885, the *Hyde* sailed from New York for San Francisco. A lofty ship, she crossed three skysail yards. As she neared the Equator, she lost both her fore and main topgallant masts in a sudden squall. Captain Pendleton, that master canvas carrier, thought little of the mishap and managed to refit the big ship at sea. He rounded the Horn on the 59th day out, and reached San Francisco on June 27th, 123 days out.

The *Hyde* now loaded 82,234 centrals of wheat at the rate of 27s. per ton. She sailed October 29th, rounded the Horn 47 days out, crossed the Line 75 days out and reached Liverpool February 2, 1886, 96 days and 6 hours from San Francisco. Discharging her cargo in excellent condition, she made the return crossing, against westerlies, to Sandy Hook, in an amazing run of twenty-two days. It was this fast maiden voyage that brought fame to the *Hyde,* and from then on she was a favorite with the shippers. It is doubtful if she could have made such a record under any master who was not a sail carrier.

A hard ship, she only made the RED RECORD after her eighth voyage, and the last with Captain Phineas in command, in 1892-3. On arrival in San Francisco the mate was charged with "breaking a seaman's wrist with a belaying-pin, and otherwise mistreating him." The facts were easily proved, but the case was dismissed on the grounds of "justifiable discipline."

Voyages nine and ten were under command of Phineas Jr., and while better than the average of other vessels, it was evident that the "boy" was not the driver his father was. On her 11th voyage the ship was under command of Captain Colcord, and made an unusually long passage for her, of 132 days to San Francisco. It was immediately surmised that Captain Colcord was not a driver, but he proved otherwise when he sent the *Hyde* from San Francisco to Honolulu in 1897, in 9 days, 4 hours and 30 minutes.

☆   ☆   ☆

If the *Henry B. Hyde* was the finest full-rigger afloat, at least under American registry, I. F. Chapman's *A. G. Ropes* was a close second for that honor. Launched in 1884, the same year as the *Hyde,* the 2461-ton *Ropes* was never in trouble of any sort. This happy state of affairs was due to the marvelous skill and fine character of Captain D. H. Rivers, who commanded her throughout her entire career as a sailing ship.

Captain Rivers was a model master, but he had one failing, if it can be called that. He was a sail carrier of the Pendleton class, and every passage of the *Ropes* out and home round the Horn maintained an average for speed that was the envy of deep water men everywhere.

One run was made from San Francisco to New York in 95 days; a trip seldom done under 100 days. From Yokohama to

Tacoma, the score was 24 days, a record for any craft. This was in 1887, with a cargo of tea. Although the *Hyde* and the *Ropes* never found opportunity for a race, and it is not easy to form an opinion as to which was the smarter ship, old hands gave the *Hyde* an edge in regards to speed.

Captain Rivers was a true Cape Horner in the tradition of keeping a ship spic and span, the gear stowed Bristol fashion. Decks, paint work, the tops of the houses were continuously cleaned and oiled, brasswork polished, rigging repaired and tarred, sails mended, yards ranging from thirty-five to ninety feet in length scraped aloft — and the *Ropes* had twenty-one. Work of this sort, carried on aloft while the ship is under way, is enough to tax the nerves and stamina of any sailor. Nor did Captain Rivers leave inspection of the work accomplished to the mates. He often went aloft himself, as high as the skysail yard, a dizzy height for man or boy.

The pins and sheaves of every block aboard were brought aft for inspection, and every foot of rigging passed through his hands. "We are painting the ship today," he wrote once. "White inside, and the lower masts pumicestoned so that they are as smooth as a table top."

Time certainly didn't lag aboard the *A. G. Ropes*.

MISTER PERRY TAKES THEM IN

Speaking of Sail Carriers, the experience of Fred Perry, Down East mate and author, illustrates the dangers in bending on too much canvas.

Mister Perry was mate of the *St. Nicholas* at one time, Chapman and Flint's 1799-ton ship, Captain Joy, commanding.

The *St. Nicholas* and *St. John* were sister ships, built in 1869-70. Tough, full-bodied square-riggers, steady-going as a pair of plow horses, they were built for one purpose — the carrying of cargo. Neither designers, builders or owners had intended otherwise and the ships themselves were quite aware of their limitations, and content to find their proper place in the maritime scheme of things.

Yet these same two vessels seemed to exert a most peculiar influence on their masters, and they each had several. The minute a captain boarded either, something apparently hap-

The 'Constitution'

Because her timbers and planks proved exceptionally resistant to shot in battle, the frigate *Constitution* was nicknamed *Old Ironsides*, and the name has stuck to her ever since. She is probably the most famous naval vessel in American history. The painting is by Marshall Johnson. *(Chrispix Archive)*

The 'Benjamin Sewall'

After building some 70 vessels at their yards in Middle Bay, the Brunswick Pennells rounded out their activities in 1874 with the building of their largest ship, the 1,433-ton *Benjamin Sewall*. The ship was built for the Sewalls of Boston, who owned the majority of the shares in the vessel; and it was their wish that she be named for one of their number, then in his 80s. (*Chrispix Archive*)

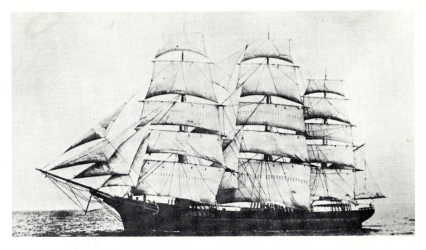

The Ship, 'C. F. Sargent'

The innocent festivities aboard the *C. F. Sargent,* which had slid down the ways in the Blanchard yard at Yarmouth in 1874 and had been named for the Yarmouth shipbuilder, Cyrus F. Sargent, were like the Mardi Gras that precedes Lent. The tidal wave that struck the guano islands within hours brought sudden tragedy, following a celebration of farewell they could not know would for some be final. *(Chrispix Archive)*

Cyrus F. Sargent

Maine vessels were often named for living State of Mainers. As a result, the name of an individual who otherwise would never be known outside his own area might literally be carried to the ends of the earth. In some instances, the names of these individuals will always be associated with the exciting stories of often incredible adventures in which ship, officers, and crew became participants. Such was the case with Cyrus F. Sargent, Yarmouth shipbuilder, whose 1704-ton ship, the *C. F. Sargent,* will long be remembered. *(Chrispix Archive)*

The Ship, 'R. B. Forbes'

Capt. Robert Bennet Forbes eventually owned a financial interest in more than 70 vessels. Four of them bore his name. One of these, the 756-ton ship, *R. B. Forbes*, built in 1851, was active in the California trade. *(Chrispix Archive)*

Robert Bennet Forbes

Being captured by the British three times before the age of nine; going to sea at 13; and working up to the command of the *Canton Packet* by the time he was 20, was but the beginning of Robert Bennet Forbes' exciting achievements.

(Chrispix Archive)

A 'Jackass Barque'

They called the *Olympic* by many names. On the Register she was entered as a "four-mast barque," but some mariners called her a "fore-'n'-aft schooner chasing a brig"; others, a "jackass barque," the latter two having reference to her mixed ancestry. She was built at Bath in 1892 by the New England Shipbuilding Co. for Capt. W. H. Besse, and was listed as a 1402-ton ship, approximately 225 feet in length, 42 in breadth, and 22 in depth. The photo shows her after being dismasted during a terrific gale, re-rigged "with single topgallant sails, and no main skysail." *(Chrispix Archive, from "The Down Easters," by Basil Lubbock, courtesy of Brown, Son & Ferguson, Ltd., Glasgow.)*

The Wreck of A Former Beauty

The peerless *Henry B. Hyde*, launched at John McDonald's yard at Bath in November, 1884, was deemed the finest Down Easter ever built. In 1884, however, coming under the management of Flint & Co., and being put in the "black diamond" trade, her usual good luck changed. During February, 1904, she stranded on Damsbek Beach, Virginia. Although floated, she again went on the beach, this time to stay. After some months, the wreck broke in two, and the remains had to be dynamited. *(Chrispix Archive, from "The Down Easters," by Basil Lubbock, courtesy of Brown, Son & Ferguson, Ltd., Glasgow)*

Mutiny on the 'Thayer'

When Capt. Clarke, after being stabbed repeatedly by the mutineers, fell inside his cabin and lay in a pool of blood, his assailant left him for dead. His plucky wife, however, now came forward and put a revolver in her husband's hand. His wounds bound up and strength returning, together they stood off the attacks of the crazed coolies. *(Chrispix Archive)*

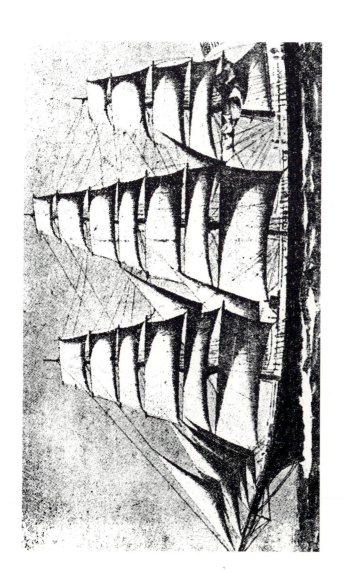

The Blood Ship, 'St. Paul'

Although named after the great apostle to the Gentiles, the 1,894-ton *St. Paul* earned a bad reputation by the sadistic methods used by her captains and officers in handling her crews. As though conscious of her guilt, she seems like a branded criminal out of some maritime Newgate Calendar. The *St. Paul* was built at the Chapman yard at Bath in 1874. (*Chrispix Archive, from "The Down Easters," by Basil Lubbock, courtesy of Brown, Son & Ferguson, Ltd., Glasgow*)

The 'Henry B. Hyde'

The *Henry B. Hyde*, described as "immensely lofty," and considered "the finest Down Easter ever built," was launched from John McDonald's slip at Bath in 1884. McDonald had worked under Donald McKay, builder of the greatest of the clippers, and something of McKay's genius had rubbed off on him. One of the four vessels owned by the Searsport captains Pendleton, Carver, and Nichols, she became a favorite among shippers in the Cape Horn trade because of her speed. *(Chrispix Archive)*

The Bloody 'Gatherer'

A number of Down Easters came to be called "hell ships," but the *Gatherer* outdid them all. Built at Bath in 1874 by E. & A. Sewall, she came in time under the command of Capt. John Sparks, assisted by a bucko mate named "Black" Charles Watts, whose exceptional sadism was even celebrated in verse. After two suicides and one murder during a single voyage, the law of the land at last intervened. Sparks was relieved of his command; Watts was sentenced to prison. *(Chrispix Archive, from "The Down Easters," by Basil Lubbock, courtesy of Brown, Son & Ferguson, Ltd., Glasgow)*

The 'Joseph B. Thomas'

Seldom have a ship and a master been so closely identified in marine annals as have the 3,000-ton *Joseph B. Thomas*, built at Thomaston in 1881, and her captain, William J. Lermond, who, like many captains of the period, had a special care for his ship because he owned a good portion of her himself. Over and above his personal concern for the safety of his ship, Capt. Lermond would tolerate no brutality aboard his vessels. *(Chrispix Archive, from "The Down Easters," by Basil Lubbock, courtesy of Brown, Son & Ferguson, Ltd., Glasgow)*

Capt. Lermond and Son

Capt. William J. Lermond was captain, and his son was chief officer, of the *Joseph B. Thomas.* Capt. Lermond was one Thomaston skipper who would allow no bucko mates or their sadistic methods on his vessels. Lermond was part-Irish, part-Maine Indian, and all-American. *(Chrispix Archive, from "The Down Easters," by Basil Lubbock, courtesy of Brown, Son & Ferguson, Ltd., Glasgow)*

The 'St. Paul' (1833)

Three Down East merchant vessels bore the taxing-to-live-up-to name, "St. Paul." One of these, a Bath-built ship, achieved a reputation as a hell-ship. The vessel shown, however, "adorned and beautified" with a life-size bust of the great Apostle as a figure-head, so impressed the natives when she was moored in Manilan waters that, when passing beneath the figurehead in their boats, they would devoutly make the sign of the cross. (*Chrispix Archive*)

The 'Nightingale'

While the 1060-ton clipper *Nightingale* was under construction just across the Piscataqua from Kittery in 1851, it was her builder's intention to name her the "Jenny Lind," after "the Swedish nightingale," whose name was then on everyone's lips. Another builder, however, had beat him to the name, so he compromised by calling his ship, the *Nightingale*. Like her namesake, she evoked admiration wherever she appeared. *(Chrispix Archive)*

The 'Frank N. Thayer' (I)

When Capt. Nathaniel Lord Thompson began to build the 1,220-ton ship, *Frank N. Thayer* (I) at his yard at Kennebunk in 1869, he had no way of knowing that this ship would give its identical name to a second vessel, built in 1878 for the same owners. Nor could he know that as a result of a gruesome mutiny aboard the *Frank N. Thayer* (II), the second vessel would receive a baptism of fire. The first was sold to a German firm in 1877, and renamed the *Doris*. *(Chrispix Archive, courtesy of Charles E. Lauriat Co., Boston)*

The 'Benjamin F. Packard'

One of the most famous carriers of sail around the Horn, this 2130-ton ship was built at Bath in 1883 by the firm of Goss, Sawyer & Packard. In 1894, her management was taken over by A. Sewall & Co. In these earlier years her officers were so rough on her crews that she became known as "The Battleship of the American Merchant Marine." The ship herself, however, outlived not only her bruisers, but her contemporaries, and was sold into an honorable retirement to a collector of marine antiques. *(Chrispix Archive, from Maine Historical Society)*

The 'Aryan'

By a rare coincidence, the *Aryan*, the last wooden "ship" to be built any-where in the world, was fashioned in the same town from which, in 1607, the first vessel to be built by Englishmen on the North American continent was launched. The 2,000-ton *Aryan* was a beautiful ship, with white-painted hull and blocks, and gleaming with polished brass fittings. At the close of the year 1918, while at sea loaded with a cargo of tallow and flax, she met her end by fire. *(Chrispix Archive)*

Charles V. Minott

With the building of his first full-rigged ship, *Tiger*, in 1860, Charles V. Minott was on his way to fame as the greatest of the Phippsburg shipbuilders. He rounded out his long career with the distinction of having built "the last of the 'Down Easters'; the last square-rigged deep-sea wood ship built in the world; and the last vessel of this type to be operated in general trade on the Seven Seas under the Stars and Stripes"— all of which has reference to his last ship, the *Aryan*. *(Chrispix Archive)*

The 'Alfred D. Snow'

While carrying a cargo of grain, the 2,075-ton ship, *Alfred D. Snow*, sprang a leak off the coast of Ireland. On becoming wet, the grain began to swell, forcing open some of the seams of the hull. The great vessel soon foundered. The *Snow* was built in Thomaston in 1877. *(Chrispix Archive)*

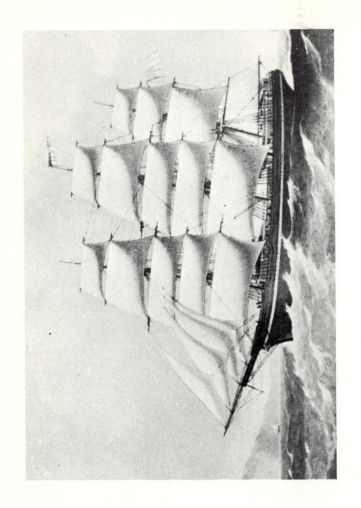

The 'Little' 'Edward O'Brien'

One of the prettiest of the O'Brien fleet, this 1,552-ton ship, built in 1863, came to be designated the "little" *Edward O'Brien*, only to distinguish her from another larger vessel of the same name, a 2,057-ton ship built in 1882. Both slid down the ways at Thomaston. (*Chrispix Archive, "A Town that Went to Sea," by A. L. Packard, courtesy of the Falmouth Publishing House*)

pened to his vision. Instead of seeing his new command as a work horse, he beheld a long, sleek-lined racehorse — and acted accordingly. Regardless of his former status, each of these captains became the wildest of canvas carriers. For more than thirty years they "drove" the aging Bath ships, and only unusual ruggedness of construction kept them afloat.

The *St. Nicholas* sailed under Captains Thomas G. Williams, William Tobey, Joy and C. F. Carver, with the flag of one partner, Old Ben Flint, flaunted aloft. The *St. John,* under Captains J. F. Chapman and O. H. Falls, boasted Chapman's burgee at the truck. The resulting friendly rivalry was good for business and brought favorable publicity, but the two vessels took jaded views of circumstances that could turn mild-mannered masters into Simon Legrees.

These two ships could not possibly compete with the sharp ships in speed, yet the driving, sail-carrying captains managed to maintain an exceptionally steady passage record. The *St. Nicholas* had a slight edge over her sister; for fifteen runs to San Francisco she averaged 138 days. Her best run was 110 days to Liverpool, in 1881, loaded with grain.

This then, was the vessel aboard which Mister Perry sailed as mate, and this was the vessel that was caught aback in the Gulf Stream Squall.

As always when she sailed from New York for San Francisco, the *St. Nicholas* was spotless and shipshape. Her master and officers were the best available, her crewmen all experienced sailors who voluntarily maintained a high standard of discipline. Forty-eight hours out, she ran into the usual Gulf Stream weather. Mister Perry had the deck for the first watch, but he was not unduly alarmed. He knew his job, and was on the conservative side. Pacing the quarterdeck, he studied the weather; the sudden bursts of wind, the lightning flashes, the heaviness of the air.

When suddenly a black cloud rushed upon the tossing ship out of the west, Mister Perry ordered the royals furled and the light staysails hauled down. Then, as it was the end of the watch, he handed over to the second who came up the ladder at the stroke of the bell. He went below and turned in. He was just dozing off when he heard the Captain's voice. "Who took the royals in?"

"Mister Perry, sir, just before he went below. Said he expected the squalls to come heavier."

There was a moment of silence. "Have them reset at once, Mister," the Old Man ordered. "Our mate seems to be timid about carrying sail at night."

"Aye, aye, sir. Reset the royals, sir."

The mate, from his bunk, listened to the second bawling the orders, the rush of booted feet over the deck. In disgust, he turned his face to the bulkhead and went to sleep.

Not only was Mister Perry aroused rather abruptly from his troubled slumber, he was hurled from his bunk and across the cabin, bouncing off the table in passage and coming up hard against the far bulkhead, bringing down gear and garments from the pegs when he struck. He shook his head to clear it, and realized at once that what he feared and prepared against had come to pass. The ship was caught flat aback!

"All hands on deck! All hands on deck!" There was a note of panic in the call, and an awesome sense of futility in the strange motionless hang of the big ship, as if between the roaring sea and eternity, as indeed it was.

The hands had tumbled out before the call and now the heavy seaboots were pounding overhead in a turmoil of shouts and the most frightening thumps. In the darkness, Mister Perry groped his way topside and up the ladder to the quarter-deck, in time to see the Old Man, axe in hand, frenziedly hacking the halliards of the royals, topgallant sails and topsails from the mizzen rigging to the fore fife-rail. He stared aghast as the headsheets and stay-sail sheets were let fly.

"Mister Perry, don't stand there. Do something," the Old Man yelled.

Mister Perry went into action. The courses were clewed up. The big ship continued to gradually heel over until she was on her beam ends. All the Captain's axework had no effect, for the backed yards kept the sails from coming down. Perry rushed to give the helmsman a hand; straining, they hove the wheel hard up, then hard down. It had no effect on the ship's head. The wind was billowing the topsails with a sound like distant thunder, the blocks of her fore-and-afters banged and thrashed, the cut rope ends streaming leeward. It was evident

now that the weary old *St. Nicholas* was about to turn-turtle. No ship, no matter how she was handled, or how sturdy, could take what she was taking and live.

Just as the Captain sang out, "Axes to the deadeye lanyards," the wind died abruptly. The ship trembled all over, like a runaway colt after coming to a halt. There was a horrifying pause — then she righted herself; the yards came crashing down, and with them a downpour of rain.

It had been a dangerously close call. After the blow was over and the repairs made, and the ship once more on her course, Perry wondered if the Old Man had learned his lesson, or would he go on canvas carrying? A canvas carrier was like a habitual drunkard; even with the best of intentions it is difficult for him to mend his ways.

He got the answer to his unspoken question when he took the first watch.

"Mister Perry," the Old Man said. "Were I you, with night coming on, I'd take in plenty of sail before turning over."

Chapter Eleven

BULLY CAPTAINS AND BUCKO MATES

To KEEP A great ship sailing in the last of the clipper era, and the long years of the Down Easters, required officers who were willing and able to enforce a discipline that was almost on a par with that of the old-time Royal Navy.

This was due to the fact that Yankees were not signing on as foremast hands, as in the earlier times; at least, not in any number. Money could be made in other and easier work, and a sea-going career didn't seem as attractive as before the Civil War.

Now the crews were nearly all "foreigners," but the master and officers were still Yankees, and usually Mainers. As the foreigners to a Maine ship officers' mind were of an intelligence level slightly below animals, and as there was little time to explain an order, the officer would "show" the willing, but rather stupid crewman with the toe of his boot or ready fists. The apparent stupidity was generally due to lack of English, yet the ship had to sail. Thus the Bully and Bucko came into being.

☆　☆　☆

"The best time to kick a man is when he's unconscious — he's more relaxed then, with less danger of permanent injury."
Mister True, of the *Edward O'Brien II*

Captain "Zack" Allen was said to be one of the meanest, toughest and hard-fighting masters in the entire Cape Horn fleet. His first mate, who was also his son, was a chip off the old block. As the son was a six-foot "Bucko," rougher, tougher and meaner than his pa, it wasn't difficult to maintain discipline aboard Captain Zack's command.

Not being a hand to take chances in such matters, Allen had for a second mate a very unruly character named Turner, who was as handy with his dukes and delighted in "rough house" as much as Junior. Unlike his superiors he did not confine his efforts toward discipline to shipboard, but to every waterfront

where the ship touched, especially the San Francisco waterfront. He made a habit of pushing through the swinging doors of a seamen's hangout, spreading his big feet firmly on the sawdust covered floor, looping his thumbs through his belt and bawling at the top of his voice, "I'm the best fighting man on the Coast. Any lubber with a contrary opinion, step forward."

As might be expected, considering the time and place, there were any number of gentlemen present with contrary opinions — and they all stepped forward. Mister Turner would then have a busy few minutes, and although he got "E" for effort he never won, for even a superman or second mate of a hell-ship has his limitations, and often there were as many as twenty-five or thirty, all brawny.

Mister Turner did have a hell-ship to be proud of, for it was not only constantly making the headlines, but more often than not was the lead story in the RED RECORD, supplement for the newspaper of the Seamen's Union. And by the way of the press, it gained the descriptive nickname, "The Battleground of the American Merchant Marine."

The name of this fabulous carrier of mayhem? It was none other than the great skysail-yarder built and owned by the Bath firm of Goss, Sawyer and Packard, the *Benjamin F. Packard*, a 2130-ton ship that helped make the United States speed mistress of the seas. Built in 1883 and named after the third partner of the firm, she was the finest of their fleet.

Today one wonders at the coincidence of so many Bath-built, owned and operated vessels that were known as "Hell Ships." The *Packard, St. Paul, Susquehanna* and Bloody *Gatherer* were merely a few of the more noted.

Captain Allen and his officers were tough, but they didn't go in for sadism. They were brutal objectively, to maintain discipline and work the ship properly, and it can be surmised because they liked to fight. It seems that they always had a crew glad to oblige, and despite the constant uproar and battle aboard, the captain, his officers and crew were expert seamen and together made some remarkable passages in their favorite "heller," the best, eighty-three days from San Francisco to New York in 1892.

Captain Allen was in command of the *Packard* for fifteen years. A most peculiar fact, considering his reputation, was the

ease with which he obtained a crew.   The hardest characters
were drawn to the *Packard,* as by a magnet.

☆　☆　☆

The *Commodore T. H. Allen,* 2390 tons, was the largest ship
built in 1884, aside from the *Hyde* and *Ropes.*   She was the last
vessel by T. J. Southard of Richmond on the Kennebec.   Perhaps the firm established by that grand old man lost heart
when they read of what was taking place aboard.

A beautiful ship and a sweet-sailer, she was named for "Old
Man Allen," the famous San Francisco stevedore and leader of
the Forty-nine Society.   Her figurehead was his carved portrait,
full length, the only one in existence that was smoking a cigar.
She had every quality a ship should possess, except for the cigar,
and she soon had a world-wide reputation — a terrible reputation.   Not only was the *Allen* a Hell Ship, she was also a "Blood
Boat."

Her master, who was responsible for her reputation, was
Captain R. L. Merriman, a genius in his profession, who made
other Bully Captains look like pantywaists by comparison.   He
had this fine ship throughout her life and it is impossible to account for his behavior.   It was claimed that Bully Sewall was
sadistic, others were tough while some were just drivers, but according to the records, Red and otherwise, the only term that
actually describes Merriman is ferocious.   It was the raw
ferocity of the savage beast, they reported, so unreasoning that
it cannot even be classified as brutal.   He made money for the
owners, and so was kept on.

Merriman, his chief mate who was also his son, Robert, his
second mate, "Big" Crocker, and the third, official "blower and
striker," were equally ferocious the seamen claimed.   To ship
aboard the *Allen,* they said, was like becoming a crew member
on a vessel commanded by four homicidally insane apes.   Together they made her the worst hell ship sailing the seas, and
no hand would sign on unless he was tired of life, or drunk.

That was the only way Merriman gathered in a crew;
through the boarding house crimps and knockout drops, and he
never had the same crew twice.   Between 1889 and 1894, the
ship was reported four times in the RED RECORD.

"When the *Commodore T. H. Allen* arrived at San Francisco in April of 1889, an A. B. named McDonald complained

to the authorities that 'whilst expostulating against the vile language of the third mate he was struck several times by that officer, and was thrown against the rail with such violence that his shoulder was dislocated.' When he complained to the captain, that kindly gentleman remarked, 'Serves you damned well right.' He then ordered the unhappy McDonald confined to the carpenter's shop, and for treatment of his wounds 'was given a large dose of salts.' "

McDonald got a lucky break. It must have been one of the quarterdeck's good days. Perhaps the third repented of his unusual lenity, for one night, staggering out of a waterfront dive, McDonald was set upon, beaten, robbed and tossed into the gutter.

☆ ☆ ☆

When the three boarding house crimps brought the usual load of drunk and drugged misfits aboard the Hell Ship shortly before sailing time, they expected it to be an ordinary business transaction. Captain Merriman would pay the fee for each shanghaied man, which in turn would be deducted from the victim's wages. It was common procedure and the only way Bully could sign a crew.

This time was different. "Sir," the mate said. "We are three men short." On a ship as big as the *Allen* this was cause for concern. The hard stares of the captain and his mates made the crimps suddenly uneasy. "What about those three?" Merriman wanted to know.

"You can't do this to us," the chief crimp shouted.

"Why can't we?" Merriman asked.

The crimp's desperate gaze roved the circle of brawny officers. "We know too much."

"About what?" the Captain asked silkily. "You brought a crew and we paid your fees. If any law-breaking was done, it was by you. Now, minded for a change of scene, you are signing on for a voyage."

"We're not seamen," the crimp protested.

Merriman grinned. "Mister Crocker will show you the ropes. You'll learn fast."

And so, like the lowliest of waterfront scum or wharfrats, the crimps got a taste of their own medicine. Crocker not only showed them the ropes, but the rope end. He was easy on them,

due to past business relationship. He might have used knuckle-dusters or his boot. They didn't fare so well with the crew, who resented their past activities.

When the ship arrived back in New York in October of 1889, Fred Hall, a greenhorn, complained of being shanghaied aboard by the San Francisco crimps. A newspaper report of the case said: "Upon complaining to the first mate and attempting to see the captain, he was driven forward with kicks and curses. He was accorded cruel treatment on the passage to New York, and when he asked the captain for his pay he was told there was nothing due him — the crimps had received all the advance and blood money. The third mate gave him fifty cents to pay his ferry fare across the river."

When the *Allen* arrived in San Francisco during August of 1892, Edwards the negro cook charged Mister Crocker the second mate, "with hitting him on the head with a belaying-pin because he allowed the crew to warm themselves in the galley." According to the RED RECORD, Crocker afterwards tried to gouge out the cook's eyes as he lay on the deck, then the first mate kicked him as he lay there, and finally Captain Merriman made him wipe up his own blood.

Seamanship and neatness were Merriman's only commendable qualities. He did like to keep things spic and span.

On the *Allen's* arrival back in New York, June, 1894, an able seaman, Charles Heyne, charged the two Merrimans with assaulting him while he was at the wheel. "The first mate beat me with a rope end," he said, "and the Captain used his fists."

Captain Merriman was arrested and held in fifteen hundred dollars bond, but the case, like that of the unfortunate cook's was dismissed for "lack of evidence."

At the turn of the century some more thoroughly determined wretch decided to put an end to the "blood boat." He set her on fire, and in November of 1901 the hulk was condemned.

Afterwards repaired and cut down to a barge, she ended her days in humdrum existence under the name of "Sterling."

One quality that Yankee Bucko Mates had in common was pride in their ship. It was their ruling passion, and they would go to any length to keep her smart-looking. Shipshape and Bristol fashion was the watchword, aloft and below, and if a Maine mate drove his hands far past the point of endurance, he likewise drove himself.

That often was the reason for his brutality. Because he was strong and able, and willing to endure for the sake of the vessel's reputation, he expected the hands to be of the same mind and just as able. When they weren't he tried to make them so. The masters usually encouraged this pride of ship on the part of the mates, for it was to their advantage to command craft to which an owner could point without flinching.

One eager Bucko formed the habit of sending both watches aloft on quiet moonlight nights to scrub the yards with sand and canvas. Another Jonesport Bucko was addicted to the between decks, which he kept always holystoned and oiled. The stringers were painted in alternate stripes of white and baby blue, then were hung with a lining of canvas. When the cargo was unloaded, this canvas was taken up, scrubbed and put away until the next was due.

The decks, especially, were always a great source of worry to a Downeast mate, and it took a lot of work to satisfy him as to a proper surface. To bring this about was a backbreaking task. First carefully holystoned and oiled, then completely coated with coal tar which was later scrubbed off, they came up pure and white as the driven snow. And if any absent-minded hand was careless with tobacco juice, or splashed paint, he caught hell with bells on.

It was this anxiety over their decks that often turned calmly severe mates into raving madmen, as was the case of Mister Beal, a Downeaster aboard a Down Easter. The name of the vessel remains unknown, but through the years the incident has furnished writers of sea fiction with plot and background color.

Mister Beal loved his decks, and the least hint of a mark or discoloration would be reason enough to break out the work

gear and turn the watch into scrubwomen, as was pointed out
often by a sea lawyer among the crew. Only the fact that Beal
was a Bucko kept them in line.

Perhaps the sea lawyer had been hitting the bottle, or perhaps he was naturally mean; most sea lawyers were. Whatever
the reason for his behavior, he evidently blew his top. Although
it was his watch below, he came on deck during the mate's
watch, one cheek bulging with a cud of chawing tobacco, one
hand lugging a bucket of slops.

The mate spied him instantly and stepped to the guard rail
to see that the bucket was emptied in the prescribed manner,
without spotting the deck. The sea lawyer saw him and grinned
evilly. He sent a thin brown stream of tobacco juice to the base
of the mizzen mast, then upended the bucket on the deck.

For a long moment the shocked watch and the mate stared
in speechless horror at the desecration. With a frightful roar
the officer leaped the rail, grabbed the frightened offender by
the throat and proceeded to use him for a mop. He next dragged
the hand to his feet and, with well-placed blows, cut him to
ribbons. The sea lawyer fell to the deck unconscious, but Mister
Beal wasn't finished. He stomped the man until he wearied,
and until the beautiful white deck was running blood and gore.

Maddened before, the sight of this mess turned the mate
into a real maniac, and his screams brought the captain, the
second and the off watch tearing up the ladder, but he drew his
revolver and held them off, then jammed the muzzle in his
mouth and squeezed the trigger.

Holystone and scrub as they might, the crew never could
get the stains out of the deck.

☆   ☆   ☆

In 1874, Albert Hathorn of Bath built the *Gatherer*, a fine
1509-ton five-topgallant yarder. Jacob Jensen was the owner,
and under her first master, Captain Thompson, she was like any
other ship in the Cape Horn trade, and only made the news by
way of shipping reports.

When Captain John Sparks assumed command, with Charlie
Watts as first mate, it was something else again. From a staid
and hardly-noticed cargo carrier, the *Gatherer* not only made
the newspapers but the front page of every one, while the

presses turning out the RED RECORD were forced to work over-time.

Compared to the suddenly soaring "reputation" of the hitherto mild-mannered *Gatherer,* all the other famous hell-ships might have been missionary boats, officered by Sunday School teachers. For the *Gatherer* under Sparks and Watts was a murder ship, with decks that literally ran with blood, and soon she was known the world over as the "Bloody *Gatherer.*"

A crowd was usually on hand when the *Gatherer* docked; reporters and photographers, a United States marshal, officials of the Seamen's Union and members of various civic groups. They came expecting the worst — and they were never disap-pointed. On every voyage "accidents" were reported in the log, and numerous breaches of "discipline." Seafaring is a hard life, and this was a hard era; when a man signed on aboard a sailing ship he was expected to take his chances on being roughed up a bit. However, with the growing number of sui-cides reported during a voyage, the authorities, pushed to it by lurid newspaper accounts, began to wonder if maybe something wasn't wrong aboard the Bath ship.

Something was definitely wrong; Captain Sparks and Bucko Watts, and they actually got away with murder for some time, until Mister Watts, arrogant and disdainful of world opinion, carried his pitcher once too often to the well of brutality.

It was on a passage round the Horn to San Francisco that the first Squarehead committed suicide. A big, slow-moving, yet willing Swede, he finally broke under the mate's steady perse-cution. Half crazed from the abuse, both physical and verbal, he began his climb to the royal yard, shouting down curses and insults to the two shocked tyrants on the quarterdeck.

Over the first surprise, the mate took after the scoundrel, chasing him through the rigging. "Yah!" the Swede yelled. "Murderer! Yankee hog!" As the mate, furious, reached the royal yard, the Swede ran out along the ice-coated lee yardarm and leaped into space. He struck the angry sea with a huge splash; a swirl of foam showed where he had gone down.

Wearily Mister Watts descended to the deck. "Sorry to lose us a hand, sir," he reported to the captain. "But that slob was too slow to be much good, anyway."

"Mister Watts." Captain Sparks paused in his slow pacing of the quarterdeck.

"Sir?"

"How did the crew take the suicide of the Swede?"

The mate grinned. "I didn't ask them, sir. The second tells me that they were somewhat disturbed."

"Think they'll make trouble?"

"None that I can't handle," Mister Watts scowled. "Those men are a pack of ingrates. They appreciate nothing we do for them."

"I've noticed that."

"Such ingratitude is a disgrace to humanity," the mate allowed piously. "Sir, I've been meaning to speak to you about the cook."

"What about the cook?"

"He's been passing out doughnuts to the starboard watch."

"He wouldn't dare," the shocked master gasped.

"You can't trust a Chink," the mate said. "Want I should take him in hand?"

"You haven't done so already?"

"Well, sir," Mister Watts began lamely. "He's the cook — " He broke off, leaped to the break. "Swanson, what ails you?"

Swanson, a wild-eyed Viking, surged up the ladder and through, his push taking the mate off guard. He raced aft, the helmsman jumping from his path as from a mad dog. "Murderer!" he snarled at the captain in passing. He leaped to the taffrail, stood balancing to the sway of the ship. He drew his sheath-knife.

"Mister Watts, side me," the Captain said as he moved in, and Watts came on the run.

"I bane fed-up," Swanson told them. He drew the sharp blade across his throat and fell back into the foaming wake. The two officers stepped to the rail and stared down at the head and clenched fist that showed briefly in a circle of red, then vanished.

Captain Sparks sighed. "Well, that makes another suicide for the log. Whatever got into the man?"

"Swedes are funny that way. Unpredictable."

"Two suicides in one voyage can cause talk. Even if it wasn't our doing."

Mister Watts nodded solemnly. "People are always ready to speak ill of a man. The blasted newspapers egg them on."

"It's the RED RECORD that bothers me," Sparks admitted. "They build up a story out of all proportion. The way they'll tell it, I pushed the man, after you cut his throat."

The mate stepped to the side of the helmsman. "You saw what happened; you'll bear witness?"

"Aye, sir, I'll bear witness." The man at the wheel smiled faintly.

The mate gave him a hard look and turned to the captain. "Sir, about the Chink — "

"Mister," Captain Sparks said thoughtfully. "Maybe you had better ease up on the cook. I dislike having my food flavored with rat poison."

"I don't like it, Mister Watts. Two suicides and the voyage but half over." Captain Sparks took a turn around the quarter-deck and halted to inspect the mate. "Could it be that you are over-severe with the men?"

"Only a mild discipline, sir. Give those foremast hands an inch and they'll take a foot."

Sparks nodded. "I agree that this is probably the most malicious crew we've ever shipped."

"Somebody is talking to them. I'm trying to find out who."

Sparks was interested. "Any leads?"

"I suspect that blasted sea lawyer, Clancy, if that's his real name. He's a born trouble maker."

"Clap him in irons."

"I did consider keelhauling the scum."

"You couldn't do that," Captain Sparks said. "The public is against brutality aboard ship."

"I know that, but it's a nice thought." Mister Watts peered forward. A number of hands were striding purposefully aft, led by the sea lawyer, Clancy. "Looks like trouble, sir."

"Take care of it, Mister Watts."

"Aye, aye, sir." Mister Watts stepped through the break and down the ladder to the deck. He spread his seaboots and waited, thumbs looped through his belt.

The deputation from the crew halted. "We'll be having a

word with the Captain, Mister Watts," Clancy, the spokesman
told the mate.

"Sir!" the mate thundered.

"Sir," Clancy said, the manner of it an insult.

"I will hear your complaint, if any."

"We'll be making it to the Captain and no other. Stand
aside, Black Watts."

"What did you call me?"

"Black Watts, a name well-earned by your black deeds," the
Irishman returned."

Mister Watts knocked him down. He bounced up, knife in
hand. Mister Watts drew his revolver and shot him. Clancy
doubled over, holding his stomach, blood spurting between his
fingers. He sagged to his knees, one hand searching blindly for
the knife he had dropped. The mate leveled his weapon and shot
the man between the eyes.

"I'm afraid you are in trouble, Mister Watts," the Captain
called down. He was right. Both Mister Watts and the Captain were in trouble. When the ship made port, the mate took
off for parts unknown, and Sparks gave up his command and
went into hiding. Watts was discovered in Ireland, brought
back for trial and found guilty of cruelty on the high seas. He
served a long term in Folsom Prison.

The afterguard of a ship usually stood together under all
circumstances, an actual necessity if discipline was to be maintained. It was the duty of the second mate to see that the men
jumped to obey orders, and if he didn't have the backing of the
mate, and the captain behind him, he was in a bad way. The
hands were quick to sense a weakness in the "enemy" and take
advantage of it. Therefore, a mate might hate the second's
guts but he never failed to back him, in the interest of efficiency
and for his own protection. If the hands managed to give the
second his come-uppance, the mate stood next on the list, and
possibly a full-fledged mutiny would follow.

The mates personally were seldom called upon for violence.
That was the second's department, and in due time he was a
Bucko, if only in self-defense. Yet it was a lot of power to put
in the hands of one man.

The Thomaston ship *Edward O'Brien II* had a series of Buckos, but there the similarity to other hell-ships ends, for the mate and second, officially buddies, evidently had a falling out, as indicated by the following item in the RED RECORD.

"*Edward O'Brien II* arrived in San Francisco February, 1890. First Mate Gillespie is charged with the most inhuman conduct. He knocked down the second mate and jumped on his face. He struck one seaman, who tried to interfere, on the head with a belaying-pin, inflicting a ghastly wound, then kicked him in the head and ribs, inflicting life marks. He struck another man on the neck with a capstan bar, then kicked him into insensibility. When the boatswain, ordered to assist him, failed to hear, the mate struck him in the face. Gillespie was charged and admitted to bail."

Whatever caused the trouble between the mates was a personal matter, never named by either man. The case was thrown out of court for "lack of evidence," and Mister Gillespie went back to his duties. The crew was naturally reluctant to sign on again, though many of the old faces were present when the ship sailed, due to the activities of the crimps. As the second was still in the hospital, the ship was short an officer. The Old Man then appointed a foremast hand to the post, after the Bosun refused to test the mate's temper again.

The crew thought they had it made, but the new second, after a few days of learning the ropes, leaned over backwards to please his superior and became one of the most brutal Buckos of all time. So brutal that Mister Gillespie had to order him to "ease off," or the ship would get a bad name.

When Mister Gillespie was replaced by Mister Carey, and a new second came aboard named True, conditions were expected to be different, for both men appeared ordinary enough shoreside; even genteel. This was wishful thinking, for the minute the ship cast off, both became loud-mouthed, swaggering toughs, to the concern of the captain. The *O'Brien's* masters were never over-sensitive, but they were beginning to be aware of public opinion, and more important, that of the owners.

Hardly was the ship past Sandy Hook and the pilot dropped when the crew sent a delegation aft. "With all due respect," they told Mister Carey, "Mister True, the second, is a brute, a fiend in human form, and if he isn't immediately restrained, he is likely to become a murderer."

Mister Carey stared down at the delegation, fists on his hips. "If you wharf rats think Mister True is a fiend, wait until you see me in action. By the time we round the Horn, you'll wish you had never been spawned. Now get forward!"

Mister True had been standing half way up the ladder, listening. "Sir," he said. "I'd like a word with the men."

"Help yourself," Mister Carey growled.

Mister True stepped down to the deck. He walked slowly toward the delegation. It retreated to the waist. Mister True caught up. "I'm sorry you men are put out with me. I'll tell you what I'll do. I'll fight any three of you scum at the same time. How about it?"

One man accepted the challenge, the wrong one. The hardest fighter in the forecastle, he promptly knocked the second down, then set himself to stomp. Mister True rolled clear, bounced to his feet and retreated aft. He seized a belaying-pin. The other crewmen, overjoyed by the success of their champion, rushed to his side.

Every officer has his sycophants. Mister True had the cook, steward and carpenter. While the mate looked on from above and the captain snoozed through his nap, Mister True and his assistants knocked down three men and placed them in double irons. The unfortunate challenger was dragged into the cabin and the second then kicked the unconscious man in the face and body until he was wearied of his fun.

☆   ☆   ☆

"Before you take over, Mister," the mate said, "the Old Man wants to see you."

"I'm in trouble?" Mister True asked in alarm.

"That is an understatement," the mate said, with a peculiar sort of satisfaction. "He's fit-to-be-tied."

Mister True went below and knocked on the door of the Old Man's cabin. "Come in." There was a rasp in the voice that did not promise well for the second. He squared his shoulders, opened the door and stepped in.

The Captain was sitting at his table-desk, weighted-down charts unrolled before him. He leaned back in his chair and

gave his attention to the tell-tale compass overhead, as if fascinated by what he read there. Mister True shifted his feet uneasily. "Mister True, I'm a fair man and an understanding
man," the Captain said. "I realize that in order to maintain
discipline it is sometimes necessary to be severe. But in the incident of the first watch, as of yesterday, you over-stepped your
authority."

Mister True was silent.

"You knocked down three men and put them in irons, in
the course of maintaining discipline. That was most commendable."

"Thank you, sir," Mister True beamed. He added gener-
ously, "I had some help."

"That's what I'm getting at," the Old Man said. "The
cook, the steward and Chips. Maintaining discipline is not their
province. When the Union hears of it, you'll be in trouble,
Mister True. But that isn't the whole of it."

"No sir," the second agreed glumly.

"With the help of your 'assistants' you dragged the fourth
man, who incidentally had been knocked senseless, into the
cabin, where you proceeded to kick the poor wretch as long as
you could swing your foot."

"Sir, that's the best time to kick a man; when he's unconscious. He's more relaxed then. Not so much danger of permanent injury."

"It didn't work, this time. The man is like to die. Now
hear me, Mister True. I want no more of such behavior. If
you can't maintain reasonable discipline on your own, with the
backing of the mate, I'll get someone who can. Is that clear?"

"Aye, sir."

The captain, in trying to stem the brutality aboard, had de-
feated his own purpose with this warning. Mister True, determined to prove his worth, ran the crew ragged. Men were as-
saulted with the belaying-pin every day, kicked into the scuppers
and stomped — all by one man. Off the Horn the ship leaked
badly, and the second kept the hands at the pumps, subject to
abuse, cold and wet, with no relief. Disregarding the Old Man's
protests, the mates really laid it on.

On arrival at San Francisco the crew pooled their wages
and told the authorities that they would spend it all to have the

mates punished. Those gentlemen were ahead of them; they disappeared. The enraged crewmen hired a private detective to seek them out, but they never were discovered.

Yankee shipmasters were not as a rule talkative aboard ship. With dignity and discipline to maintain, they kept to themselves, even treating the mates with extreme formality. And the mates preferred to have it that way. If a master was too friendly, it made them uneasy. Yet a captain could be eloquent on occasion, and it was the custom of many at the beginning of a voyage to call the company aft and make a little speech. This example, published by HARPER'S in 1874, in a little book written by a United States Consul and entitled AMONG OUR SAILORS, is typical.

"Men! My name's Captain Halyard. I'm master of this ship and I want to start square with you. We've got a long voyage before us and there's plenty of work to be done. I want you to understand I'm great on discipline, and you can have hell or heaven on board, just as you please. All you've got to attend to is your duty and obey orders; that's what you shipped for and that's what you're paid for. If you do your duty it will be all right; if you don't, it will be all wrong.

"The first man that disobeys my orders I'll put daylight through him — quick, and here's the little joker I'll do it with." The captain dramatically draws a revolver and holds it up for inspection. "If any of you men tries to make trouble aboard this ship, I'll make it hot for you. I'll make mincemeat of some of you quicker'n hell'd scorch a feather! . . . you've got Bloody Jock Halyard to deal with. Now you know who I am and what to expect. Go forward!"

If the above address lacked certain literary elements in its construction, it was forceful and to the point. In other words, the crew got the message.

Captain Joseph E. Sewall was a smart shipmaster and famous the world over for his handling of ships and men. In fact, not only was Captain Sewall famous; he was notorious as a Bully Captain who figured more often in the news than any other Blue Water Man. The headlines didn't seem to bother him any, and he was apt to boast of his unenviable distinction of being reported more often in the RED RECORD than any other American master, with the possible exception of Merriman of the *Commodore T. H. Allen.* Given below is a fair example of how the San Francisco RED RECORD commented upon Captain Sewall, and this newspaper opinion was shared by seamen everywhere.

"Captain Sewall is one of the most notorious brutes in charge of an American ship. This is his fourteenth appearance in the RED RECORD in less than seven years. Well sustained charges of murder have been made against him, but he has gone scot-free every time. Once in Philadelphia in 1889, when he was in danger of conviction, he disappeared for a time, and afterwards healed the wounds of the complainants with a small consideration in cash."

After reading this account and others, one might easily gain the impression that Captain Sewall was a giant, lowering brute in appearance. On the contrary, he was dapper, average in build, and a bit of a dandy in dress. He had a mouth full of gold teeth, framed by a neat, well-kept mustache and goatee beard, and it was said that he considered himself something of a ladies' man. In ordinary conversation he was soft-spoken and very polite.

Yet regardless of his qualifications, appearance and manner, every ship that Captain Sewall went master of became a hellship, and the men claimed, to see him pacing the quarterdeck, or standing at the rail beaming down at the mates who were dishing out the mayhem, was like watching Hiram K. Satan himself.

Those gold teeth came in handy to the Captain, for he was said to use them as a signal to begin the slaughter. When he flashed them in a broad smile, the waiting mates put on their knuckle-dusters and went to work. If a hand was experienced enough he took off at the first glint of pay dirt. He was invariably caught, sooner or later, for a man can run just so far aboard a ship, but if he was really rugged and his wind held out there was a faint possibility that the enraged officer would tire before he did.

On the subject of enraged officers, it didn't take much to

enrage any sailing ship mate, Bucko or not. "Mates were born mean," the oldsters claimed.

Many shipping concerns wouldn't hire a Bully Captain or a Bucko Mate. Others, money-minded, were glad to have them on the payroll, for a driver of men was always a driver of ships, and a fast passage brought quick and huge profits.

Joe Sewall was quite a young man when he took over the *Solitaire*, but it was not long before he made both his fine ship and himself infamous.

He didn't look like a villain. With his genteel manner and fastidious dress he could easily have passed for a professional man shoreside. Probably a doctor or lawyer. One certainly would not have taken him for a Bully Captain, one of the most brutal on all the Seven Seas.

His first command, the *Solitaire*, was a fine, five-topgallant yarder; a smart, fast-sailing vessel of 1532 tons. A typical Cape Horner was the *Solitaire*, with "yards and masts that shone like silver." There was a pride and dignity about her, and a sort of hopeless sadness, for she was a hell-ship and couldn't do a thing about it. Not while she was in the hands of a "monster," as the foremast hands and the San Francisco RED RECORD called her master.

Other Bully Captains were brutal in the way of business, as were many of the mates; to get work out of the hands, to make a fast passage, a name for themselves and money for the owners. But the seamen claimed that Joe Sewall enjoyed making people suffer. To stand by the quarterdeck rail, they said, to him, as he watched the mates working over some unfortunate, was better than a box seat at the best show in port.

In 1891 Captain Sewall left the *Solitaire* to take command of Arthur Sewall's second four-mast bark, the *Susquehanna*, of 2591 tons, or five hundred tons smaller than the *Shenandoah*. She was reputed to have the prettiest lines of any Sewall-built ship. Her maiden voyage to San Francisco was about average, for Captain Joe, a master navigator, was studying the capabilities of his new command. On the voyage from San Francisco to Liverpool he "drove" her, and the *Susquehanna* arrived on September 3, 1892, only ninety-four days out from the Golden Gate.

Perhaps the bark then had a presentiment of what was to come. She had no inclination to become a hell-ship. No self-respecting vessel wanted the finger of scorn pointed at her, no more than did any other female, especially when she was so pretty. She didn't want men to shun her.

On the following passage from New York to San Francisco, the unhappy *Susquehanna* found herself listed in the RED RECORD. It had been a lively voyage, but for a vessel under "Bully" Sewall's command a comparatively mild one. Nonetheless, the bark was terrified when she made port, her yards back, canvas furled and her hooks dropped. What had happened to her shouldn't happen to a dog, let alone a lady.

It was April, 1893 and the crew immediately made complaints to the authorities respecting the mate, who was, however, an honest Bucko and a real fighting officer. He didn't rely on the second to take care of an unruly seaman, and in this case had challenged the sailor to a fair fight on the maindeck, unusual procedure aboard any ship, let alone a hell-ship. Captain Sewall was intrigued by the possibilities, as was the crew.

The mate said later that he wanted to give the man, "a misbegotten limejuicer," a fair show, on account of international relations and such. Oddly enough, his non-political victim did not appreciate the concession.

First off, he told the court, he was knocked down. Then he was tumbled into the scuppers, bruised and bleeding. But was the blasted Yank mate satisfied? Blimey, no! As the beaten Britisher lay there, the mate jumped on him; not once, but several times.

This was a mild charge to bring against one of Sewall's officers, and when the mate, that fair-minded soul, explained to the judge that he had only been maintaining discipline, the case was dismissed and the foremast hand admonished to mend his ways.

Mister Ross, on having this case against him thrown out by the court, couldn't understand why afterwards the crew went out of its way to get even, for he considered himself to be fair minded at all times, even when he was "maintaining" discipline. But when the bark arrived in San Francisco from New York on November 12, 1895, the crew brought new charges against him and he was arrested for brutally beating a seaman named James Whelan.

This time the court, mildly influenced by the press, may have been inclined toward the opinion that perhaps something was wrong with Mister Ross. Captain Sewall, however, surprised and furious by the arrest of his mate — "a good man if ever there was one" — swore that if his officer was convicted he would have the whole crew arrested on a charge of mutiny. He hired the best lawyers available and the case was subsequently shifted to the jurisdiction of the United States Commissioner Hancock who dismissed it for lack of evidence.

An ungodly howl went up from the RED RECORD and the national press. Charges were made, although not officially, that undue pressure had been exerted to free the mate, by shipping interests too important in the national economy to be ignored.

All this publicity was evidently not to the owner's liking and the Bully Captain was advised to watch his step. That he took this advice is evident from the fact that no further charges were brought during the next few years against either Sewall or his officers.

In 1905, the *Susquehanna* loaded 3558 tons of ore at Noumea, New Caledonia, and cleared for Delaware Breakwater. It was a heavy cargo for any craft, even this sturdy bark, and under a severe spell of weather she was strained and her seams opened, allowing the sea to pour in from several points. Thirty men were put to working constantly on the pumps, but when on August 24, 1905, it was found that even with this number of seamen applying themselves to the task, the water could still not be kept down in the pump well, the order was given to "Abandon ship."

Chapter Twelve

MISTER MARTIN OF THE *St. Paul*

"ALL MATES have a mean streak," the Shellbacks claimed, "but some are meaner than others. These are the varmints that become Bucko Mates. Why some I've knowed would have tried to blow down their ma, while still in swaddling clothes, then kick her into the scuppers." In following this thought trend, it was agreed far and wide that Mister Martin, brutal Bucko second mate of the Bath hell-ship *St. Paul,* hadn't been born of human parents. He, the Shellbacks claimed, had been spawned by the Devil."

This, of course, was a slight exaggeration. Mister Martin was human enough, but to what extent was a matter of opinion. Actually, Mister Martin was no worse than other Buckos, and not as bad as some; Mister Ross of the *Susquehanna* and Black Watts of the Bloody *Gatherer,* for example. And one point in Mister Martin's favor was the fact that he never committed murder, nor was he ever accused of it. If he "blew a man down," kicked him into the scuppers and stomped him into insensibility, it was done objectively, in the interest of discipline and a strong sense of duty to the owners. There was nothing truly malicious about Martin, and he not only was the soul of integrity and a fine seaman, but a hard worker who drove himself hard as he drove his men.

Something else. Mister Martin had a heart of gold — if one delved deep enough to find it, had the opportunity and was quick on one's feet. For Mister Martin resented prying and showed this resentment with a heavy hand. His greatest worry was that he would lose his hard-earned reputation as a brutal Bucko. What foremast hand would jump to obey orders of a mate known to be religious-minded, with pet charities and secretly a. . . . No, this is not the time and place to let the cat out of the bag.

Mister Martin need not have worried, for when his terrible

secret did out, no one would believe it, so he went to his grave
secure in the fame he had won as a brute among brutes.

There were some who knew better; a little old lady in Aus-
tria, the Sisters who taught in a West Coast orphanage, a certain
Baptist minister who had felt the second's heavy hand, down-
and-outers who frequented the Chink's Place on the San Francisco waterfront. The list is long, but to the world at large the
sturdy Austrian-born second mate was indeed a monster, and
Mister Martin wanted it that way. But why? What was the
reason behind his ruthlessness, for there must have been one
other than shipboard efficiency? And why did the tough Aus-
trian sign on a Yankee ship in the first place? There was shipping aplenty in Europe. Was he running away from something?
It is a doubtful conjecture, for Mister Martin never ran from
trouble.

He must have learned his seamanship on the other side, for
he was an expert when he joined the *St. Paul,* and it was said
that he held master's papers. Certainly he had the capability
for command. Yet he was always remembered as a Bucko Mate
— the terrible Bucko of the *St. Paul.*

It was Mister Martin who made the *St. Paul* of Bath, Maine,
a hell-ship. Her twenty-two year old captain, Bert Williams,
while severe in the matter of discipline, was not a Bully, nor was
the mate, who is seldom mentioned in the records. Yet out of
necessity, to maintain discipline, they backed Mister Martin and
he made the most of that backing.

Heavy - fisted and knuckle - dusting, to the seamen sent
bruised and battered, rolling into the scuppers, the fact that
the second mate was anything but what he appeared to be would
seem highly improbable. They would scoff at the mere suggestion that the terrible Bucko had a gentler side to his nature, and
a well-guarded secret, that were it to get out, would be his ruin;
he would be the laughingstock of the Seven Seas. Life would
be a hell for Mister Martin then, nor would he need be on a ship
to catch it.

Like all secrets, this one did get out, but inadvertently, for
the two principals in the affair had made a bargain, and they
stuck to it. It was in later years, however, and men who had

felt the toe of Mister Martin's boot, just wouldn't credit the story. "Not if a minister told it, after swearing on a stack of Bibles," they declared. So such was the second's lethal reputation that he was able to sail serenely through the years, gently bashing heads and kicking ribs in, and leaving a wake of blood and gore for the record.

It was a minister who discovered the dark facet of Martin's personal life, and it was he who made the bargain with the mate not to make this knowledge public, and thereby blast the Bucko out of his snug berth. The man of the Cloth had reason aplenty to hate the second and wish him ill, for he had been shanghaied in a most treacherous manner, and suffered violent persecution since. Evidently he practiced what he preached, and turned the other cheek.

Due to her bad name as a hell-ship and blood-boat, it became difficult for the *St. Paul* to obtain a crew. The captain was then forced to pay the crimps a heavy toll of blood money to get hands of any sort, and they were just that. In the late fall of 1890, the *St. Paul* was lying in San Francisco Bay, loaded with grain for Liverpool. Only lack of a full crew kept her from sailing with the tide. The crimps and boarding house runners were scouring the waterfront for victims, but it wasn't like the old days. Now that the word was out even the most reckless seamen made themselves scarce.

Three famous rivals in the evil trade of crimping, Shanghai Brown, Red Jackson and Three-finger Daly, in desperation decided to let bygones be bygones and band together in the interest of efficiency. They made a wide sweep, in the manner of the old-time Royal Navy pressgangs, but for all of it the catch was puny.

Mister Martin volunteered to try his hand. "I can do better than those lubbers," he told the Old Man.

For the first time in his sea-going career, Mister Martin realized that the crimps really did earn their money. Now he stood hopelessly on Market Street, hands jammed in his breeches pockets, his roving gaze in search of prey. The street was unusually free of sidewalk traffic, as had been every dive he entered, except for a cautious bartender with a bung-starter close at hand. It was almost as if he had been expected. If only he hadn't boasted that he could outshine the professionals.

About to admit defeat, he saw a well-set-up citizen coming toward him; one who with a little training would make a likely foremast hand. As the prospect drew near, the second's pleasure dissipated like fog under a hot sun. The fellow had the round-about collar and staid black garb of a minister. It was the final disappointment to a disappointing day. Mister Martin grew thoughtful when he saw that the sky pilot was young and rugged. "Sir," he said, intercepting. "Can you direct me to the nearest seamen's mission?"

"My friend, that is a coincidence." The preacher smiled. "I was also looking for the mission. There doesn't seem to be one in this area, where it is definitely needed."

"Reverend, it certainly is," Mister Martin agreed piously. "The first place I make for in a new port, is the Bethel. This is my first call here." He brightened, as if struck by an idea. "Why could not some of us followers of the Lord get together and form a mission; right here on Market Street?"

"I've long had such a thought in mind," the preacher said.

"Let's go to a place of refreshment and talk is over," the second suggested, as he led the way to the nearest saloon.

"I've never been in a place like this before," his new friend told him.

"It's the logical place to find sinners; people who need saving," Mister Martin pointed out. "I divide my time in port between the mission and these dens of vice. Well, Reverend, what'll it be?"

"A glass of milk."

"Milk?" The bartender recoiled in horror.

"Milk," Mister Martin reaffirmed flatly, giving him the eye. "I'll take a glass of cold tea."

"I'll see what I can do," the man in the apron said.

"Here's to the good work," Mister Martin toasted, when the refreshments came, lifting his glass of tea. "Down your milk, Reverend, then we'll talk business."

When the minister came to, he had a splitting headache. The floor was swaying, and the ceiling too, with a peculiar creaking sound. He lay on his back and tried to figure it all out, but he was weary, so he turned over on his side and dozed off again.

He was roused by a kick in the ribs that brought him sitting. Relieved to find his Market Street friend, Mister Martin, standing over him, the minister smiled and said, "Somebody kicked me, unless I dreamed it."

"You didn't dream it," Mister Martin said, and kicked him again.

The shocked minister pulled himself to his feet. He stared wildly about. Even to his befuddled mind it was evident that the swaying floor was actually a pitching deck; that the creaking sounds were straining timbers, and the wash of water proof that he was aboard ship. "What is the meaning of this outrage?"

"What outrage?"

"I've been shanghaied."

"That's gratitude for you." Mister Martin looked sadly upward. "You get raving drunk, I bring you aboard to sober up, and you claim to be shanghaied."

"We're at sea."

The second nodded. "Well outside the Golden Gate. The ship sailed with the tide. I had to bring you along, or leave you to sleep it off in the gutter. That wouldn't have looked well to your congregation."

The minister shivered. "You can't get intoxicated on milk. I was drugged." He was suddenly aware that his clerical garb was missing; that he was clad only in worn dungarees and a tattered jersey. And he was barefooted. "Where are my clothes?"

"They were not suited for the work you'll do."

"I won't work. I'll complain to the captain."

Mister Martin cast aside his genial mask. His fist, on the jaw sent the preacher back to the deck. He gave him the boot.

"Stop! I'm a minister of the Gospel."

"Minister or saint — hell! Up you get and work." Martin grabbed his new foremast hand and frog-walked him up the ladder. "You sky pilots are always talking about hell, but it was all guess work. At the end of this voyage you'll have first-hand information."

The crew were pleased to have the minister forward; his

presence made life easier for them. Mister Martin was like a
child with a new toy; he spent most of his time persecuting the
parson. Yet despite the abuse, the Man of God learned fast.
By the time the ship was down to Cape Stiff, he could furl the
skysail with any man.

The Baptist clergyman attended a rough school under a
hard master, and he grew strong in the process, able to hold
his own with the forecastle bullies. But not with Mister Martin,
who had Authority behind him. Fate, however, was working
slyly on the minister's behalf.

It was close to the middle of the first watch when the young
Old Man mounted to the quarterdeck, cocked a weather-eye aloft,
studied the horizon and spoke tersely to the mate, who in turn
shouted down to the nearest hand, the shanghaied minister.
"Tell Mister Martin he's wanted on the deck."

"Aye, aye, sir!" The minister went below and along the
passage way to the second's cabin. As he raised his fist to
knock, the roll of the ship unlatched the door. It swung open —
to reveal the terrible Bucko perched on the edge of his bunk,
busily knitting a lace doily!

The minister stared, speechless. Mister Martin stared back,
also speechless. He had turned pale, the needles frozen in his
nerveless fingers.

The minister found his voice. "Sir," he faltered, fascinated
by the dainty bit of lace in the big, toil-hardened hands. "The
captain sent for you." From his reading and talk among the
crew, he knew that shipmasters often had hobbies to pass the
lonely off-duty hours. Some were religious-minded, some wrote
for the newspapers, read classics or made ship models. Captain
Andrew S. Pendleton was a proud maker of net lace; he finished
a bedspread each voyage. Not to be outdone, Captain David A.
Scribner's specialty was macrame lace, while others did oil
painting. But the Buckos were not usually given to hobbies, unless it was breaking heads. And here was the most brutal of
them all, knitting a lace doily.

Mister Martin carefully folded his knitting and tucked it
under the mattress. He examined the knuckles of first his right
fist, then his left. "You aim to tell the crew?" he asked mildly.

"Tell what, sir?" The minister met the worry in the second mate's eyes without flinching. He tried not to, but he couldn't help grinning.

"You tell and I'll beat the life out of you," Mister Martin said.

"By that time the damage would be done," the minister pointed out.

Mister Martin nodded. "What kind of a deal do you want?"

"Only that you ease off on me for the rest of the voyage."

"Fair enough," the second agreed. "I have your word on it?"

"Just one thing more. I want you to read the Lord's Prayer until you can repeat it backwards."

"That's pretty brutal," the Bucko Mate allowed. "Where is your Christian charity?"

"You just heard it, sir." The minister stepped through the opening. "Thank you, sir."

"O. K. It's a deal," Mister Martin said hastily. "You drive a hard bargain for a sky pilot."

Both men kept their word. The *St. Paul* made a fast passage, 101 days to the Mersey. In Liverpool the minister cabled his friends in San Francisco for passage money home. Although he could have signed on the *St. Paul* for the return voyage, he didn't want to press his luck.

☆　☆　☆

Many were the yarns told of the fabulous Mister Martin, and most of them were on the violent side, but here is one with an amusing twist, and it too happened in San Francisco.

The *St. Paul* was loaded and due to sail with the turn of the tide. As usual, Mister Martin had worked hard overseeing the stowing of cargo and on other duties, many of which were not his own. But Mister Martin was an eager-beaver, a glutton for work. He took little pleasure shoreside, except by occasional visits to the Bethel, or a dram or two with a friend in a Market Street grog shop. He was definitely not a drinking man.

It was the Old Man himself who advised Mister Martin to take off the few remaining hours before sailing time, to relax. "You've been working too hard, son," he said, although the second was ten years his senior. "Be off with you."

"Are those orders, sir?"

"They are, Mister Martin," the captain said. "Take off and lively now."

"Aye, aye, sir." So Mister Martin went shoreside and wandered along Market Street, jostled by the sidewalk crowd and not resenting it. He felt lonely, and for the first time was appalled by the realization of just how alone he was. "Nobody cares whether I live or die," he mused as he stared morosely at the fog-dimmed lights. He sauntered along until he reached the Chink's Place. He paused, then turned in. He nodded at the owner who was helping behind the bar, then slumped into a chair at one of the small tables. He ordered a beer. When it came, he peered sadly into its remaining head. "My life to a T," he muttered. "All froth."

"Do you mind?" A slender figure took the opposite chair. "The other tables are crowded."

"Not at all," Mister Martin said politely, glancing up. He met the startled gaze of one of his foremast hands, an inoffensive little character named Perley Groot, who, stranded on the coast, had signed on to work his passage back to Maine, and home. "You should be aboard," Mister Martin said. "We sail with the tide."

"Sir, I'll go aboard right now." Perley's voice was frightened. He rose.

"Sit down, lad," the Bucko said genially. "We'll go together, after I buy you a beer." He wasn't taking any chances on a hand getting away. "Fill mine up again," he told the barman. "And one for my friend." He eyed Perley over his second mug of foaming suds. Maybe he had a friend after all. Leastwise, he had someone to talk to. "Tell me about yourself, boy."

Perley knew Mister Martin's reputation and he was scared nearly witless, but under the warmth of the second's smile he opened up. He told the terrible Bucko of his hopes, his dreams, of his sweetheart back in Lubec. He was flattered by the second's undivided attention, even if it did make him uneasy. "Sir, let me buy this time."

Five beers later, listening to the story of the young Maine boy's life, Mister Martin became dully aware of another presence. It was "Black" Watts, one of the worst Buckos on the seas, who drew up a chair and sat down. "Hello, *St. Paul*," he grinned. He gave Perley a fishy stare. "Ain't you lowering your standards, somewhat?"

"Perley is my friend," Mister Martin explained ponderously. "My dear, dear friend." A tear welled out of his cold blue eye and rolled down his cheek. "Perley is a good boy."

Perley, frightened by the fast company he was in, suggested, "Sir, hadn't we better be getting back to the ship?"

"All in good time," the second said drowsily. "First we'll have another beer."

"I'll buy the next round," Black Watts offered, grinning evilly. So this was the famous non-drinker?

The mate of the *St. Paul*, worriedly pacing the quarterdeck, cast frequent glances dockside, hopeful that Mister Martin would show before sailing time. The Old Man didn't hold with tardiness, especially from an officer. When he finally spied the second inching along the dock, supported on one side by Watts and the other by Perley, his heart sank. The Old Man didn't hold with drunks, either. But Mister Martin wasn't a drinking man. Maybe he had met with an accident. "Avast there!" he called. "Bring him aboard. Lively now!"

It was a chore, but they made it, while Mister Martin leered owlishly at his superior. "Old friend," he said thickly. "All my old friends."

Then, as Mister Martin's feet struck the deck of the *St. Paul*, a miracle took place before their eyes. He became cold sober; his old efficient self — the ruthless second mate. "What are you gawking at?" he demanded of the startled Perley. "Who do you think you are?"

"Sir," Perley faltered. "I'm your old friend."

"Old friend, hell! Get forward where you belong, you scum!" And Mister Martin helped him on his way with the toe of his boot.

Chapter Thirteen

MUTINY

IN JANUARY OF 1886, the 1600-ton ship, *Frank N. Thayer* was homeward bound from Manila with a cargo of hemp for New York. The weather was fine and the winds fair, and apparently the *Thayer* was due for a favorable and uneventful passage.

On the night of Saturday, January 2nd, the big ship was sailing quietly about seven hundred miles off St. Helena. It was almost like being aboard a yacht, with little straining of canvas or creaking of timbers, the rush of the water along the sides a restful sound.

The mates, first and second, sitting chatting on a hatch cover, commented on this. The port watch had gone below and the starboard watch, as was the custom on such a night, had curled up in likely spots, bent on some well-earned sleep, but careful to keep out of the moonlight. As any seaman can tell you, it doesn't pay to sleep in the moonlight.

Captain Clark, his wife and child, were asleep in the master's cabin, aft below.

The mates broke off their conversation as two foremast hands stepped out of the shadows, directly in front of them. They were new men, signed on at Manila; natives. One belonged to the watch on deck, the other to the watch below. The mate spoke to the man. "You're in the watch below."

"That is correct, sah," the slender young islander said. "But I do not feel well." This evidently was a prearranged signal, for both sailors drew their knives and fell upon the mates. The first mate, bleeding from several wounds, staggered forward. The watch, wakened from their sleep by his screams, picked him up and ran to the forecastle; still half asleep, they were caught by panic and barricaded the door. The mate, moaning in agony, died three hours later.

The second mate, under cover of the uproar, eluded the murderers long enough to drag himself to the companionway ladder. He had been stabbed repeatedly and blood was pouring from his wounds as he slid down the ladder and pulled his weight along the passageway by the knobs of the stateroom doors. He banged on that of the master's cabin. "Captain Clark," he called. "Captain Clark!"

The Captain, roused by the screams, the confused shouts and the rapid patter of feet along the deck, rushed out of his stateroom and jerked open the cabin door. The second mate dropped dead at his feet. The man was covered with blood, but the nature of his wounds was not apparent. Captain Clark's first thought was that the *Thayer* had collided with a ship they had steadily been overhauling at sunset. In his nightclothes and unarmed, he went up the companionway ladder. As his head appeared above deck, a knife blade laid his scalp open and a muscular hand gripped his throat. Although taken by surprise, he lashed out with his fist and caught the mutineer between the eyes, temporarily blinding him.

The killer struck back with his knife, driving it deep in the Captain's side. Desperately wounded, Clark continued to fight, and fighting they rolled down the companionway. Inside the cabin, the Captain's wife, a woman of courage, put a revolver in his hand. The killer, thinking him dead, had returned to the deck. Now armed, the Captain returned to the foot of the companionway and called out to the man at the wheel to shut the door leading to the poop.

The terrified helmsman was useless in the emergency, his hands frozen to the spokes. "I can't, sir," he quavered. "Somebody is in there."

"Who?"

"I don't know, sir," the coward replied. From his peculiar behavior, and still without information as to what had happened, Clark assumed that the entire crew had mutinied. He returned to his cabin and with the help of his wife, locked the doors leading forward and aft. The wide-eyed child was told to remain in her berth, as it seemed the safest place and out of line with the skylight.

By now, the Captain was near collapse from shock and loss of blood. He was brought taut by the sound of rapid steps in the passageway. Revolver ready, he opened the door on a crack.

Seaman Hendrickson stood there, nearly crazed with fright. "Hide me," he kept repeating. He stumbled into the cabin.

The Captain shut and bolted the door. "Lot of good you are," he said. He believed himself to be mortally wounded. He sat down in a common chair, where he could command the doors, ports and skylight. Mrs. Clark set to work, for this was the first opportunity she had to dress her husband's wounds. He had a number of slashes in the head, but the most dangerous was the hole in his left side from which the lobe of a lung protruded.

Meanwhile, the nine men of the starboard watch who were barricaded in the forecastle, the first surprise of the attack over, armed themselves with capstan bars and made a sally to the maindeck. They got as far as the mainmast, where they were ambushed by the two natives. Four of the nine were stabbed, four fled forward again, and one, named Robert Sonnberg, pelted aft and climbed into the mizzen rigging to find a precarious refuge on the crossjack yard. From this perch he saw the blood-maddened natives murder Maloney, the cowardly helmsman, who begged for his life. The freed wheel began to spin lazily, first one way, then the other. The ship lost way, came into the wind, canvas slatting.

After they murdered Maloney, the Manila men tried to get into the cabin through the skylight, but two shots from the Captain drove them away. It was now about two in the morning. Sonnberg, from his exposed and uncomfortable position saw the wild men discover the hidden carpenter and a foremast hand, whom they butchered. They found two axes, which they sharpened, grinning up at Sonnberg fiendishly. Then they lashed their long-bladed knives to broom handles. So armed, they headed for the skylight again. Using the weapons as harpoons, they tried to reach the Captain. His shots drove them away.

About eight in the evening the madmen turned their attention to Sonnberg, still aloft. He was no longer unarmed, for he had cut a block adrift and now swung it at the end of a gasket. Warned by the shaking of the rigging that the killers were on their way up, as the first came within striking distance, he lashed out with his awkward but lethal weapon. Although he missed, the nearness of it unnerved the wretch, and with his mate he descended to the deck. Sonnberg, panicked anew, climbed to the royal yard, where he spent the remainder of the night.

The dawn of Sunday morning found the madmen complete masters of the ship. The Captain dared not leave his cabin, were he able. The crew could not make a second sally from the forecastle, for the mutineers had it battened down. At seven bells, feeling the need of nourishment, the natives searched for the Chinese cook, found him hiding in a coal locker, dragged him out and forced him to prepare a bountiful meal. Murder worked up an appetite. The intriguing aroma of cooking food didn't do poor Sonnberg any good, high on the royal yard, already more than twenty-four hours without food. Nor did it help the imprisoned watch or the people in the master's cabin.

The Manila men now found a real harpoon. Armed with it and their knives, they headed for the skylight, determined to stab Clark and his wife. The revolver was knocked from the Captain's hand; he slipped, fell heavily. Mrs. Clark snatched up the weapon. The harpoon slashed through her nightgown, ripped it off and gashed her from breast to thigh. Unmindful of the shock and streaming blood, she held the heavy Navy revolver with both hands and tried to take careful aim. She almost dropped it with the roar and recoil, but the grinning face of the enemy jerked back from the shattered skylight.

Being Sunday, the two natives decided to improve their appearance. They broke open the dead carpenter's chest and dressed in his best clothes. After all, Sunday was a day of rest, and while out of necessity, they couldn't take the whole day off from killing, they could relax for a few hours. For the remainder of the afternoon there was not a sound on the helpless ship. As the weather was fair, with little breeze, she sailed serenely on, a dead man at the wheel.

With darkness of the second evening, Sunday, January 3, 1886, the killers resumed attack on the cabin, but were driven off with a steady revolver fusillade. The rest of the night was quiet. At daybreak, Sonnberg, from on high, saw the villains making preparations to set the ship on fire. While they were busy at this happy chore, he also saw Ah Say, the cook, slip an

axe into the forecastle port. With the knowledge that the watch
was now armed, Sonnberg regained his courage, slid down a
backstay, found another axe and started to work on the outside
of the barricaded forecastle door.

The killers spied him and raced forward, knives flashing.
Once again he escaped aloft.

Captain Clark, despite his wounds, was feeling stronger,
due to the hovering care of his loving wife and her clever medical treatment. He determined to reconnoitre. The terrified
hand, Henrickson, he dragged from the bathroom where he had
been hiding, and for the first time learned from him the details
of the mutiny. He gave the man a revolver, and one to his wife.
With this backing, he started up the ladder.

The Manila men were advancing once more to the attack.
The Captain took careful aim and shot the leader through the
chest. The killer staggered, whirled and ran forward where
the crew was chopping a way out of the forecastle. As the
wounded native came abreast, the door smashed outward. The
furious seamen surged to the deck. "There's one," they shouted.
"Grab the S.O.B.!" The killer rushed to the rail and leaped
overboard. His mate dropped between decks.

The crew rushed aft and Sonnberg came down from aloft,
hand over hand, yelling for the Captain. As he came out of his
station on the run, trailed by his wife and Henrickson, Sonnberg
shouted, "The dastard is setting fire to the ship!"

Two seamen, armed with revolvers, rushed below. The
smoke between decks was so thick it covered the killer's movements, but they got in a shot that struck his shoulder. He
worked his way to the deck, where with a blood-curdling shriek
he leaped overboard. The killers had prepared for escape by
dropping a small raft over the side. They were now clinging
to it. The enraged crew lined the rail and held target practice,
roaring with laughter as the targets tried to dodge the bullets.

"Don't kill those men," the Captain's wife begged. "Lower
a boat and bring them aboard."

Everybody stared at the lady, whose entire side was seeping
blood through makeshift bandages. This was carrying feminine
compassion too far. "Bring them aboard so we can hang them
from the yardarm," she added.

Sonnberg touched the Captain's shoulder. "The ship's afire."

"Finish them off quickly," the Captain ordered. "Then all hands turn to for fire-fighting."

A well-directed volley ended the story for the Manila men, but the fire between decks had been well set and was in the cargo of inflammable jute. It was obvious that the *Frank N. Thayer* was doomed. The order was given to abandon ship.

One boat capsized when lowered, so everybody, with the necessary stores was crowded into the remaining lifeboat. It got away safely, but held hard-by all Monday night, in the hope that the flames would bring a rescue ship. When none came, Captain Clark set a course for St. Helena. For a sail they used two blankets fastened together. At midnight, January 10th, they reached Jamestown.

Crazed by blood-lust, two small natives had killed five good men, wounded five others and a woman, mastered a crew of twenty, and destroyed a fine 1600-ton ship. All for no apparent reason.

☆   ☆   ☆

Mutiny has always been an ugly word; it was especially so in the era of sail. And the penalty for the offense was as sure as death and taxes.

It could not be otherwise. Out of necessity, the captain's word was law. At his command, relayed by the mates and bosun, the foremast hands were expected to jump, to obey without question or complaint.

If a sailor, at the instigation of a sea lawyer, or if the sea lawyer himself dared take exception to an order, the food or living conditions, he immediately became a marked man, a target for abuse. If he continued in his disobedience, and was on an ordinary ship, he was put in irons for the rest of the voyage. If the dissident character happened to be aboard a hell-ship, he seldom got so far. And if he managed to survive until port was made, and complained to the civil authorities, the cards were still stacked against him, for his complaint was usually dismissed for "lack of evidence." Or the judge would rule that the "alleged" acts of brutality were but necessary discipline for protection of life and property, and to work the ship.

The RED RECORD finally aroused public opinion in favor of more humane treatment for the foremast hands. Before the "Reformation" a ship's officer would often overstep the bounds of propriety, as in the case of the Thomaston captain who shot several drunken and unruly seamen. He made the mistake of calling at a French port directly after the incident. The French did not approve of such behavior and the shocked shipmaster served a prison term and paid a heavy fine.

The ship's officers were not always in the wrong. As a rule, they were within their rights, and in a case of actual mutiny, their actions were justified in law. This was well illustrated by the mutiny aboard the *Young America*, one of the most famous clippers.

Captain H. T. Baker was in command of the sleek, one hundred forty thousand dollar ship, with the long bow and racy appearance. He had been in command from her twentieth voyage in 1876, and was to hold it until her last but one, in 1883.

Baker was not a brutal captain, but he was as firm as he was considered just, and very severe to hands who got out of line. Even so, when the crew mutinied and stormed the quarter-deck, he tried to reason with the malcontents.

All were armed and determined on trouble. They shouted him down and spreading out, came at him. One cannot but help wonder where the mates were at this time. Nor could help be expected from the man at the wheel. It was his duty to keep the ship on her course. Now he made a point of it, staring stonily ahead and aloft and down at the compass, while completely ignoring what promised to be a very gory homicide.

Realizing that further argument was useless, Captain Baker grabbed a fire axe and went to work. Evidently he was an experienced axeman, for he quickly did for five members of the mutinous crew; the others threw down their weapons and surrendered.

When the *Young America* reached Liverpool, Captain Baker was praised by the authorities and the Underwriters for the courageous manner in which he had protected the property entrusted to his care. Being a fair-minded man, Baker was prompt to point out that he was also protecting the hide of a certain shipmaster.

Chapter Fourteen

THE HARD WAY

BIG RUBE (Cut-throat) Lawrence obtained his nickname the hard way. A giant of a man, he carried a scar that reached from ear to ear, the mark of a would-be assassin's knife.

At the time Big Rube nearly became a *corpus delicti,* he was first mate aboard the *Richard Harvey,* a New Orleans cotton packet. The captain of the *Harvey* was one Bully Brown, notorious as a ruffian with sadism proclivities. He had a violent temper and was a stickler for discipline. On a previous voyage, his son, the mate, had spoken out of turn. Brown had marooned him on a barren Pacific island.

Big Rube didn't approve of mistreating the crew. He spoke up respectfully but firmly against it to his superior. Brown's reply was to grab a belaying-pin, bellow like an enraged bull, and charge his new mate. Rube side-stepped the first rush and when the Old Man began his second charge, he set himself and lashed out with the old one-two that rocked Bully back on his heels. He followed it up with a haymaker that lifted the captain off his feet and slammed him into the wheel, making it necessary for the stony-faced helmsman to straddle the body in order to maintain his steering.

Bully crawled out from under and shaking his head, pulled himself up. He came lurching in again, swinging wildly. Rube realized then that the hassle would continue all night, unless he put an end to it, so he did, giving Brown the beating of his life in the process, to the pleasure of the assembled crew.

Vowing revenge, Brown secretly hired a "Spig" among its members to take care of Rube on the first dark night. The hired killer made the attempt that nearly took off the mate's head, but he never collected his money. Rube, blood spurting from his wound, bashed in the man's head and threw him overboard.

Brown was rather concerned over the failure of his revenge attempt, but consoled himself with the fact that he had saved the murder fee and could use the same money to hire a second killer, unless the mate left the ship at the end of the voyage. It was Brown's standard boast that no mate dared sail a second voyage with him, but Big Rube didn't follow the pattern. Despite his butchered throat and realization that the captain would do his best to complete the job, he signed on again.

It became a sort of deadly game between them, the crew betting on the outcome. Bully would hire his killers and they would simply vanish from the ken of men. Finally, frustrated and disheartened, the terrible old man had to admit that he was beaten.

Cut-throat Lawrence became a byword in ports the world over. He was later mate of the famous 2046-ton ship *Triumphant*, a three skysail-yarder and sister ship of the equally famous *America*. He was next named master of the Sewall-built 3288-ton *Acme*. A big man in every way, Captain Lawrence retired in 1906.

"Dinky" Bunker, mate of the *C. F. Sargeant*, was a little cuss, who weighed only one hundred thirty-five pounds. As might be expected, any number of foremast hands and water-front toughs tried to take advantage of that fact.

Any uninformed "hardcase" who laid violent hands on the little mate, however, soon regretted his hasty action, for Dinky was the lightweight champion of Maine, and without too much effort could knock a six-foot, two hundred pound seaman clear across the main hatch.

To the initiated, who had learned the hard way, it was always fun to watch a swaggering new hand come to joyful attention when he first spied the runty mate, smile wolfishly and spit on his knuckles. They would then place bets as to how long it would take Mister Bunker to teach the muscle-bound one the facts of life aboard the *C. F. Sargeant;* twenty seconds, or ten.

Mister Bunker was not a Bucko. He was mild-mannered and soft spoken, like so many professional fighters. He was an expert seaman, and as mate, was ever ready to give a greenhorn a hand. He frowned on profanity and excessive drinking, although he was not a spoil-sport. He would go out of his way to avoid trouble, but when it was unavoidable, he would take care of it.

When some new hands signed on at Portland, the crew spotted a broad-shouldered, loose-lipped individual, with a complexion that bespoke very mixed ancestry, among them; a potential trouble-maker and would-be forecastle boss. Under any other mate they would gladly have taken him in hand, but this was the *Sargeant*, with Mister Bunker as mate. The ship had hardly rounded Cape Elizabeth, when the expected happened.

The mate snapped an order. The watch jumped to obey; all except the trouble-maker. He ignored the order.

"You, there," the mate called. "Give the others a hand."

"Who says so?" the new hand wanted to know.

"The mate of this ship," Mister Bunker explained gently.

Big Mouth looked around. He saw the grinning crew. He didn't know that they were grinning at him. "I don't see no mate," he said. "All I see is a boy telling growed men what to do."

Although he was watching the little officer in eager anticipation of the coming fracas, he didn't see what hit him. Slammed hard to the deck, he was dazedly trying to cipher it out when the mate reached down, grabbed a handful of his shirt and dragged him to his feet. The mate cuffed him a few times, then brought up a haymaker that sent him rolling into the scuppers.

The officer stood over him. "I'm Mister Bunker, the first mate," he said, by way of introduction. "When you address me, say 'Sir.'" He nudged the fallen hero with the toe of his boot. "Now go about your work."

The recently educated hand scrambled to his feet, "Aye, aye, sir. Thank you, Mister Bunker, sir."

☆   ☆   ☆

Difficult as it often was to sign on a crew in the sailing ship era, and especially aboard the hell-ships when the crimps and boarding house runners came into the picture, it was sometimes as difficult to sign them off.

By custom, crews were signed on for the voyage; at the end of the voyage they were paid off. However, there was no law that said they couldn't sign on again for the next voyage, and immediately on arrival. If they happened to like the ship and her officers, many of them did, and remained technically aboard while she was discharging and taking on cargo.

The owners discouraged this procedure, for it ran up a steep wage-and-found bill. If the vessel was in port for any length of time the expenses of an unnecessary crew would cut the profits to an alarming scale.

It was therefore the duty of the mates to drive the non-active crew away, once it had been paid off. Several methods were used; some genteel, others exceptionally brutal.

The chief offenders in this respect were the so-called "Souwegians" or "Squareheads." Fine seamen and neat, although somewhat clumsy when aloft, shipmasters should have offered inducement to keep them aboard. Homefolk, the Souwegians didn't like change. When they found a ship where the food was edible, the forecastle comfortable, and mates who only occasionally gave them the boot, they tarried.

The Buckos, naturally, had little trouble with lingering hands; they couldn't get away quick enough. But mates with a sense of decency were up against it. Mister Blunt was of the latter type. First he tried the power of suggestion. It worked with all but the Souwegians; big, mild-mannered men, but stubborn. Blunt began to lose his temper. He hazed them until they were half crazed, but still they hung on. Finally he had a brilliant idea.

One morning, as the skeleton crew were washing the decks, he sent the Souwegians aloft. It was just sunrise. As they reached the main royal yard, the mate stood on the roof of the deck house and drew his revolver. "Now then," he shouted. "Crow like roosters and flap your dratted wings. Lively now!"

The unhappy six, perched on the main royal yard, flapped their arms and crowed "Cock-a-doodle-do" to the amazement of the hands below and the dockside workers.

Ridicule did the trick. The Souwegians went ashore with their duffle and stayed until they were shanghaied again.

In the era of the Down Easters, the great Maine ships of maritime history, a good cook was worth his weight in gold, and usually he freely admitted it. Moreover, he was apt to be a sea lawyer, and one very demanding. And when the ship was out from port, he became arrogant. Yet regardless of his personality, his unruly or obnoxious behavior, if he was capable and turned out bountiful and tasty meals, the ship's company, from the captain on down, would put up with him. Sometimes, though, a cook did go too far. . .

As a cook, "Bellerin" Blanchard filled the bill and then some, but as a person to be closely associated with, day after day, with the voyage stretching far into the future, he left much to be desired. A big, rugged character from Rockland, Maine, with fists the size of hams and a readiness to use them, he also had a mean streak that made him constantly in search for a reason. A deeply religious man, he was extremely vocal in what he thought was a musical way, and was forever singing his favorite hymn, one then at the peak of nautical popularity.

What "Bellerin" did to it was brutal, and whenever "Throw Out the Lifeline, Someone Is Sinking Today" rose above the sounds of clashing pots in the galley, everybody wanted to take off, but there was nowhere to go, except over the side. And it's said a few even contemplated that. As if to rub salt in a raw wound the cook would boast that both words and music for the hymn were written by his friend, the Reverend Edward S. Ufford, Baptist preacher, lecturer and evangelist, who for many years conducted the Bethel Mission, near Snow's shipyard at Rockland.

Never able to understand why he was not allowed to sign on for a second voyage, Blanchard moved from ship to ship, dishing up meals fit for a king, then with his rendition of "Throw Out the Lifeline" giving the crew dyspepsia.

At New Orleans he signed on the *Richard Harvey* at the time its aforementioned Captain, "Bully" Brown was engaged in his deadly feud with the mate, "Big Rube" Lawrence. The cook was presently approached by the captain with a tempting offer to poison the mate's food, but being, despite his vocal and other shortcomings, a basically honest man, he refused.

Whether Brown was fearful that the cook would inform Rube of his offer, or whether he couldn't take the hymn any longer, is a moot point. Several crew members later darkly suggested that Brown was responsible for what happened, but they could have been trying to cover their own guilt. The fact remains that when the cook fell overboard, or was pushed, and yelled for a lifeline, there was delay in heaving it — and the sharks got there first.

Chapter Fifteen

CAPTAIN FIVE BY FIVE

CAPTAIN EDWIN T. AMESBURY, one of the best known of the Blue Water Men, was short, but exceptionally broad. And any hopeful individual who attempted to take advantage of his diminutive stature, soon realized that he had made a horrible mistake, providing that he was able to realize anything after the Old Man went into action. For in his prime Amesbury weighed two hundred and twenty pounds, all brawn and muscle. To tangle with him was like taking on a buzz saw, sided by two mean and ugly catamounts.

Amesbury wasn't a Bully Captain; he was friendly, mild-mannered and soft-spoken — unless riled. Then he would clear the deck of a vessel, a waterfront pub, or the main street of an offending town, like a modern bulldozer run wild.

Born at North Haven April 3, 1837, he started his seafaring as a boy of fifteen aboard the ship *Borodino*. A hard worker and quick to learn, he soon fought his way to the quarterdeck, and it was a fight. When he was named second officer the crew thought they had it made, for the friendly boy had been so busy in studying that his fighting prowess hadn't been tested. To the general surprise, he had no trouble at all in maintaining discipline. Not after a few battered and bleeding hulks were carried between decks for medical attention.

From second mate of *Tullulah*, brig, he went to the bark *Richard*, then was made first mate of the schooner *Snow Squall*. His first command was the *Katahdin* brig. He then went as master of five schooners and later in command of another brig, the *C. S. Packard*, in the West India and South American trade. His first big command was the bark *Jennie Harkness*, launched at Camden, Maine, in 1879. He had the 1373-ton vessel for ten years, then took over the *S. D. Carleton*.

The 1788-ton *Carleton* was a fine ship and perfectly sparred, but she evidently spread too much canvas. Her mainyard was ninety-six feet long, and unlike most American ships she carried double topgallant sails. Rounding the Horn February 10, 1890, she ran into a rip-snorter of a gale and all the topgallant masts went over the side. Amesbury was somewhat disturbed by this, but what really annoyed him was the fact that it took a whole month of battling to make the westing 50°s. On April 14th the Equator was crossed. After a weary run against head winds, the great Carleton and Norwood full-rigger entered the Golden Gate, following a passage of 151 days.

Captain Amesbury was completely mortified, but he maintained his usual stony calm on the quarterdeck, which didn't fool the crew. They jumped at his slightest command and it was said, although not proved, that the first mate paled when he spoke.

Shoreside, where the shipmasters gathered to talk shop, the "slow" voyage of the *Carleton* was the topic of much humorous conversation. Everybody smiled so Amesbury wouldn't mistake the good-natured banter for something else, not wanting to spend off-time in the hospital. Sugar-coated or not, it was bitter medicine for him to swallow.

It was Captain Jim Murphy of the Bath ship *Shenandoah*, the only man with nerve enough, who added the wormwood and gall. "Ed," he said gently, "there's only one way to save your reputation and that of the *Carleton*. A race. Under the circumstances, I'll be glad to give your slow ship a day's head start."

"James," was the quiet reply, "that won't be necessary. We'll clear together."

Wagers were made on the spot, and the news spread like wildfire. Everybody everywhere got up his cash and even the Underwriters entered the picture.

☆　☆　☆

Both ships were evenly matched and both were launched in 1890, the *Carleton* a 1788-ton full rigger, the *Shenandoah* the pride of the nation, a picture of the remarkable four-master engraved on the registers of all craft flying the Stars and Stripes. She had cost one hundred seventy-five thousand dollars to build and spread more than two acres of canvas. By her rig called a four-masted bark in Britain, a shipentine in the United States, her marvelous speed and sailing qualities were due directly to the expert supervision, during construction, of Captain Murphy, who had been called from the quarterdeck of the *Babcock* for the purpose.   He also supervised the rigging of Sewall's first four-master and the stepping of her masts, an important task in any vessel.   "She handles like a knock-about sloop," Captain Jim was fond of saying, "and a full point closer to the wind than the best."

The race was from San Francisco to Le Havre.   Loaded with the biggest grain cargo on record, 112,000 centals, about 5300 tons, worth the cost of her building, the *Shenandoah* cleared the Harbor on an August morning of 1891, in company with Down Easters *S. D. Carleton* and *M. P. Grace*, and two British ships, *Strathearn* and *Balkamah*.   All were bound for Le Havre except the *Grace*.   She was for New York.

The betting odds on the two big Maine ships were about even, with a slight edge in favor of the Sewall ship.   After the tugs cast off, Amesbury tacked the *Carleton* to the north'ard. Murphy headed south.   Although they did not meet again until the end of the race, the two Mainers, when later the logs were compared, found that they were never more than fifty miles apart all the way down the Pacific to the Equator.

It was close, but the *Shenandoah* won.   Averaging 278 knots for twenty consecutive days, she reached Le Havre, November 18th, 109 days out.   The *Carleton* docked on the 21st, 112 days out.

The race must have been what the *Carleton* needed, for the bad luck of her maiden voyage didn't hold.   She made several fast passages to Australia.   It was returning from one of these, outward bound from Melbourne in 1895, in rounding the Cape, that the ship was pooped by mountainous seas.   One made kindling of the wheel house, smashed the wheel and carried the compass overboard.   Of the two helmsmen, one had his arm broken, one was knocked out, while the mate, George W. Hatch, was killed.   Nothing was left of the wheel but the upright standard, the hub and shaft.   It looked like Davy Jones' Locker, yet the crew didn't panic with Captain Edwin T. Amesbury in command.   First off, he clamped two heads of beef tierces over the wheel hub, then he cut up capstan-bars for spokes and strung them together with rope to form an improvised rim.   He made a steering compass by fixing an old compass card to a spindle on top of a soap box, held in the socket by leather, reinforced by lead in heavy weather. This homemade compass he checked by the tell-tale compass above the chart table in the cabin. By it he was able to navigate for the two-thousand mile voyage.

In 1896, the *Carleton* ran into more trouble, going ashore on Panjang Reef, Java, while bound from New York to Shanghai. Amesbury got her off without salvage tugs, but the big ship was leaking so badly she had to put in to Singapore. Then the *Carleton's* luck turned again, when that same year she made a fast and profitable passage from Sydney to London in the wool trade. At the turn of the century the ship was bought by the California Shipping Company for the timber trade. In 1906 Amesbury retired, and long after, at eighty-four was as apparently spry and bright-eyed as in his happily violent youth.

He always attributed his health to the fact that he had never spent a cent on medicine in his life and had steered clear of sawbones and their probing ways, a statement he made with his characteristic chuckle whenever a doctor was present.

Chapter Sixteen

CAPTAIN JAMES F. MURPHY

THE GREAT CAPTAIN JAMES F. MURPHY was born in Bath, March 31, 1850. He came by his love for the sea naturally, for his father, James K. Murphy was a famous shipmaster of his day, sailing out of Bath throughout a long and distinguished career. His mother, before her marriage, was Mary Jane Sewall, of the old shipbuilding family. Jim as a boy lived in a house on Green Street, attended the public school until thirteen, when he persuaded his father to let him join the *Australia* as cabin boy in 1863.

The ship was sold at Fort Adelaide. The elder Murphy returned to Bath, but the son shipped as foremast hand aboard a New Bedford whaler. He returned to Bath at the end of the voyage and to please his father entered High School. He survived that humdrum existence for two weeks and then made his escape in the schooner *Orville*, jointly owned by his father and Frank O. Moses. The schooner was wrecked on Scatarie Island, on a passage to Cape Breton. All hands were saved by climbing to the tip of the jibboom, then dropping to the surf-pounded rocks below.

Instead of this washing away his desire for a seafaring life, Jim took the experience as part of the day's work, and after a short rest shoreside shipped out as second mate on the Houghton ship *Crescent City*, Captain Frank Delano. In the course of two voyages to the Chincha Islands, he was promoted to second mate.

Next, he sailed as mate successively in three barks managed by John H. Kimball; the *Annie Kimball, Sagadahoc* and *C. O. Whitmore*. In 1872, while the *Whitmore* was lying in Liverpool, Jim received word from a relative and former commander, Captain Lincoln, that the Searsport ship *David Brown* was at Plymouth, in dire need of a master for her return voyage, as the captain had broken a leg. He advised Jim to apply for the command.

It was good advice and Jim got the berth. However, when he stepped into the cabin, the injured skipper was outraged. "I won't stand for it," he bellowed. "They sent a boy to fill a man's shoes. I don't want this ship sent to Davy Jones' Locker."

"Nor do I, Captain," Murphy told him. "Don't you fret; we'll make out." Events proved that Jim Murphy, an "Old Man" at twenty-two, was not an ordinary boy.

Sixty-six days out of Plymouth the ship dropped her hooks in Melbourne harbor. The passage gave Jim so much confidence that he took it upon himself to charter the ship from Newcastle to San Francisco with a cargo of coal at thirty-two shillings, sixpence per ton, and from there to Queenstown with wheat at eighty shillings, which figured roughly at twenty-eight dollars a ton for a six months' voyage. The owners were delighted by this example of business ability combined with professional skill. The *Brown* was but a temporary command, but at the home port of Searsport the owners offered him a ship, and as an added inducement promised to throw in a Searsport bride.

This was flattering and pleasant to a young man, but Jim was not being pressured into a hasty decision. Yet he had an open mind, although it was more'n half made up. He liked the ship first-rate, and the young lady candidate for his favor was all that was claimed for her, and more. He liked the cut of her jib, high bows and graceful lines and she had a well-modeled stern, gently rounded, instead of squaring off like some. But she had a slightly flighty look; would she be able to hold her canvas under stress and stand up under storm?

Actually it was a purely academic question, for when Jim Murphy returned to Bath he marched straightway to the home of Elisha Higgins, and once inside popped the question to Miss Maria, the prettiest girl in town. He hardly hoped the luscious creature who had beaus trampling each other underfoot would say "yes," and he nearly lost his sea legs when she did. Finally he got his bearings with the realization that his prospects had settled down to an even keel. All he needed now was a command.

He got it in the new ship *Alexander*, Alfred Lemont owner. The wedding took place in 1874, and the honeymoon voyage was two years long.

The ship called at many strange ports, and as Jim always expected the worst in such places, he wasn't surprised at what took place at Mollendo, a port at the extreme southern end of the Peruvian coast. The fact that it made him the central figure in a near-international incident didn't bother Jim in the least.

As the waters were tricky thereabouts, both Jim and the mate were on the quarterdeck, close to the helmsman, when the big ship felt her way in, leadsmen in the chains. Suddenly they spied a cutter racing out from shore, and assumed it to be a pilot boat. When it drew alongside and a line was passed, the Mainers were fairly dazzled by the quantity of gold braid that came up the ladder. "I, senor, am the Port Captain," a pompous little Latin in a comic opera uniform told Jim. "I will examine your papers; yes?"

"Senor, you will examine my papers, no! Nor are we yet in the harbor."

"Let go the anchor," the Port Captain ordered sternly.

Forty-eight fathoms was no anchorage. "No anchor," the Bath captain said. "Where is the pilot?"

"No pilot. Let go the anchor."

Jim ignored him and the ship continued on her course. At the proper anchorage, Murphy let go his hooks.

"You will hear more of this," the Port Captain warned darkly. The Americano had proved too smart and had cost him the twenty-five dollars usually demanded for moving a ship that anchored improperly to the identical berth the *Alexander* was now in. He went down the ladder to his cutter without saying goodbye.

He tried again that very afternoon, coming up the ladder in frock coat, striped trousers and top hat. "Haven't I seen you before?" the astonished Murphy asked.

"I, senor," the visitor said, with a low bow, "am the acting American Consul. I will now examine this ship's papers."

"Before you examine the ship's papers, I'd like to see your own — as Acting American Consul," Murphy said.

The diplomat was flustered. "Senor, I deeply regret that they are not available. I came away in such haste . . . "

Murphy scowled and the "Consul" recoiled. "Mister Larkin, escort this gentlemen to his boat."

"Aye, aye, sir," the mate replied, reaching for the now frightened visitor.

"Jim, dear, weren't you rather harsh on that little man?" his wife protested. "He could make trouble."

Captain Murphy grinned wolfishly. "I can double-match him there."

☆ ☆ ☆

On May 2, 1894, a Peruvian holiday, a boat put out from shore, came alongside and demanded a line. It was passed, the ladder dropped and a six-foot Negro in a dazzling uniform climbed to the deck. "Where de Yankee captain?" he shouted.

"The captain is on the quarterdeck," the mate said. "You mind your manners."

The Negro stared at him insolently, put a silver whistle to his lips and blew it. Two soldiers, carrying rifles with fixed bayonets, popped over the rail. "Out of mah way, white boy," the officer snarled.

The mate nodded to the bosun, who also had a whistle. He piped "all hands" and in a twinkling the deck was crowded with annoyed Mainers, most of them armed.

The two soldiers looked uneasy, but the Negro was already mounting the ladder. "Sah," he informed Captain Murphy importantly. "This is the Anniversary of our Great Nation's Independence. The Port Captain directs yo' to dress the ship in honor of the Day, forthwith."

Murphy had been called from a task of breaking cargo in the hold. He was in no mood for celebrating foreign holidays or holding chit-chat with uppity local officials. "Get," he ordered, and the boarding party got.

The curt refusal brought two cutters filled with soldiers alongside. The Port Captain, in a gold-braided fury of patriotic indignation, came over the rail. As official representative of the great nation of Peru, he would dress the ship himself. If the Yankees interfered, it would be at their peril.

The time was past for talk. Captain Murphy took the Peruvian Authority by the scruff of the neck and the seat of his tight-fitting pants — and tossed him into the harbor!

As Mrs. Murphy had feared, the situation then deteriorated rapidly, to the point of being very "sticky." All the Mainers were prepared to die to the last man for the honor of Old Glory and the Pine Tree State.

Then like the climax of an old-time melodrama, the U. S. S. *Omaha* steamed into the harbor, guns bristling eagerly. It had come to help celebrate Peru's Independence Day, and it promptly took the situation in hand. Later, in company with her commander, Captain Murphy visited Lima, told his story to the American minister and soon Mollendo had a new port captain.

☆   ☆   ☆

Captain Jim often said that he could "feel" a ship, once he had her a few days at sea, and this he had proved with his favorite, the great *Shenandoah*. For a ship is a living thing, and to the mariners, each had a personality, an intelligence of her own. And like humans, ships have peculiarities. Some are set in their ways, and more than a few were given to tantrums on occasion. It was then that a ship needed a master with a strong hand, who was firm, yet understanding. With a good ship this understanding was mutual, and this is why Captain Jim and the *Shenandoah* got on so well together.

As Commodore for the Sewalls, it was Murphy's job to take a new ship out on her maiden voyage; to study her ways under all conditions, with view to improving rig or gear, ballast, manner of stowing cargo, or even personnel. So Captain Jim took the great three thousand ton *Arthur Sewall* to sea for the first time. He took her to England and back. He told the Sewalls, "I don't like the way she acts; she's cranky and I can't put my finger on the reason for it. All I can say she's a queer ship. I've got a family. I won't take her out again."

The Sewalls, the designers, the engineers and workmen all studied the ship as she rode complacently at her moorings. They went over her in detail, from stem to stern. They examined her building plan, the original designs. They took account of her sail plans, rigging, gear, checked the ballast. Not a thing appeared to be wrong. She was a ship to be proud of.

The press got wind of this unusual activity. What was the reason for it? The owners wouldn't talk, nor would Jim. "Boys, whatever is bothering you, there is no reason for it at all."

"Is something wrong with the ship, Captain? Will you make a statement?"

"I already have," was the bland reply.

No one ever found out what was wrong, but Captain Jim watched with a heavy heart as the ship dropped down the Kennebec at the beginning of a new voyage, and each day thereafter hated to turn to the shipping news in his paper.

The *Arthur Sewall* loaded coal in Chesapeake Bay for the Pacific coast — and was never heard from again! "Father could always tell," Murphy's daughter Jane said in later years, "if anything was wrong with a ship."

☆   ☆   ☆

In 1893, Captain James Frederic Murphy, master of the huge Sewall four-master *Shenandoah*, made the RED RECORD. Accused of making no attempt to save a seaman who fell overboard from the royal yard, Murphy's excuse was upheld by the shipmasters. "The ship, under topgallant sails was being heavily pressed. The weather was far too bad to make lowering a boat possible."

In rebuttal, the RED RECORD, while admitting the facts, bluntly stated that a "humane commander would have made the attempt."

Murphy learned of the outbreak of the Spanish-American War on a passage from San Francisco to Liverpool. Off the English coast a British tramp spoke with the *Shenandoah*. "Watch for hostile torpedo boats," its skipper called. "They are on the lookout for you."

Murphy found it difficult to credit the warning. "Sounded like he said the enemy was laying for us. What enemy?"

"Does it make any difference?" his mate asked.

Murphy studied his clenched fist. "Nor would I be the one to say so," he grinned. Another tramp steamer showed to warn him of the ambush, and took the big craft in tow until a Liverpool tug showed up.

In July of 1898, while the *Shenandoah* was lying in the Mersey, Murphy received a cable from the owners. "Insure the vessel against war risks on the passage to Baltimore." Insurance of this type was very expensive. "And if it would not save my beautiful *Shenandoah*, then it is no insurance at all. On the other hand, I am taking out insurance that will save both money and ship. So put your minds at rest, gentlemen, sirs," he cabled in reply.

So the captain whose burgee was green, bearing a golden harp without a crown, went out and purchased two four-inch guns, which he mounted fore and aft on the *Shenandoah's* deck. He cleared port with double lookouts posted and offered a prize to the man who first spied the enemy.

Sure enough, a Spanish gunboat showed and fired a shot across the Bath ship's bows. Instead of heaving-to, the *Shenandoah* continued to log fifteen knots, spreading every bit of canvas aboard. Two rounds were fired at the gunboat, which promptly sheered off, to follow at a respectful distance. After four hours it was left behind.

The *Shenandoah* had a great reputation for speed, but she was not a fast ship, her best about fifteen knots. It was under Murphy, who was daring in the extreme, that the big four-master did more than her best. But only under Murphy. She sailed primly and properly under other commanders; with him she was ready to take any risk.

☆   ☆   ☆

The *Shenandoah* under Murphy was seldom overhauled, but she was on one occasion by the *Cutty Sark*, Captain Woodget. It was January 25, 1895, when the *Sark* came boiling up, the bone in her teeth. Murphy was somewhat irritated by the fact that the great four-master could be overhauled by a little full-rigged ship; and in Cape Horn weather. He was mortified. "What ship is that?" he signaled.

"This is the *Cutty Sark*, London bound," her master sang out. "Would you like a tow?"

Murphy exploded. When he made port he vowed to look Captain Woodget up and explain a few things.

One of the *Shenandoah's* most satisfying victories was her race against the White Star four-master *California*. A fine craft, she left San Francisco ten days ahead of Murphy's big command. She was overhauled on a Sunday morning, with the wind freshening fast. She had all three royals furled, but the *Shenandoah* roared past under full sail.

Yes, Captain Murphy had a knack with ships and he never hesitated to put his trust in the mighty *Shenandoah*. And she, being a real lady, if a rather lively one, never let him down. They came to a parting of the ways unexpectedly, a discouraging and saddening event for both ship and man. It was in 1898, when Murphy was ordered to Santiago de Chile to supervise repairs on the big ship *Kenilworth,* which had put in under distress.

Murphy could not forget the *Shenandoah,* and she seemed to lose her zest for life under other masters. In 1902 they were together again, when he took her from San Francisco to Liverpool and back to New York. She was like a new ship in her happiness. It was only for one voyage. From 1902 to 1910, she was under command of Captain O. E. Chapman.

A lucky ship, she had one unlucky passage. Clearing from Baltimore in 1907 with 5400 tons of coal for San Francisco, Chapman decided to go by way of the Cape, instead of the Horn, as he was doubtful of his all green hands. Eight hundred miles east of Good Hope the ship ran into a stiff westerly gale that, due to the heavy cargo, strained her. When she became suddenly sluggish, investigation showed her half full of water and leaking badly. By manning the pumps night and day she was kept afloat and course was changed to Melbourne. She lost seven new sails by the incompetency of the crew, many of whom had never been to sea before.

After repairs, the *Shenandoah* resumed her voyage. Nervous under the mishandling of her greenhorn crew, she ran into more trouble, running aground on the treacherous shoals of Potato Patch, December 26, 1907. Her leaks started again and soon the water in the holds was six feet deep. Pumps brought the water down and tugs got her off. Towed to Mare Island, she was pumped dry and her cargo of coal discharged. Put in drydock, she was given an extensive overhaul.

The greatest blow came in 1910, when she was sold to Scully of New York for a paltry thirty-six thousand dollars, for conversion into a coal barge! She, the marvelous *Shenandoah,* darling of the American people and beloved of Captain Jim Murphy, with her picture on every ship register and on the license of every master, doomed to spend the remainder of her days in the wake of a smoke-belching tug.

Murphy was sent out to bring her back, and they made her final voyage around the Horn together. Perhaps, just perhaps, the *Shenandoah* might have thought, in rounding the Horn, they would go down together. But both she and Murphy knew that it couldn't be; they had too much integrity to take the easy way out. So they made the final passage in good style, even as in the old days, and to see the famous *Shenandoah* rounding Sandy Hook under full sail, one would never guess that the end was so near.

This voyage did give the four-master courage to face up to what lay before her, and for a few years she suffered the degradation of being towed up and down the Atlantic coast with coal in her holds. It was her war effort; in 1917 everybody was expected to do their part. Finally, shortly before the close of the War, the *Shenandoah* couldn't take any more of the dreary service; the last in line behind a self-important tug. And it can be assumed that she was thinking of Captain Jim Murphy when she foundered off Shinnecock Bay, Long Island.

Murphy had other ships; for two voyages he took over the *William F. Frye,* a big four-master and the last vessel Sewalls built for their own use. Then he handed her back to Captain Joe E. Sewall and "retired" from the sea.

Back home in Bath, Murphy could frequently be seen gazing hopefully down the Reach, as if he expected to see the *Shenandoah* under full sail, making port.

☆　☆　☆

Captain Murphy was not only Commodore of the Sewall fleet; even in retirement he was their trouble-shooter. If he couldn't solve a problem connected with ships or shipping, nobody could. Thus when the firm's ship *Kenilworth,* bound from Hilo, Hawaii to New York, caught fire in the South Pacific, it started a chain reaction of such proportions that only Captain Jim could handle.

It was dreadful news to reach Bath. Both Captain Baker, under whom Murphy had served, and his chief mate had been suffocated by the thick smoke that rolled suddenly into their staterooms. The second mate took over. Mister Genereaux did his best, but he was a young man and had a mutinous crew to contend with. They had to fight the fire to save their own lives, but they didn't like the idea of two dead officers in their bunks. Dead men should be buried at sea, the crew insisted. It was bad luck, otherwise.

They already had bad luck, the second pointed out, hand on the butt of the revolver in his belt. Howsoever, if they weren't satisfied with the bad luck they had, he, Mister Genereaux would be pleased to accommodate them with a great-plenty more.

It took the ship sixteen days to make the nearest Chilean port, cargo still ablaze, the dead officers awaiting shoreside burial, and it was H. W. Grace and Company, the big shipping firm, that sent the word to Bath. "A special agent is needed immediately to handle the ship's affairs, to advise the mate, a young man among the South American political wolves, gathering for a feast of Yankee dollars."

"Mister Arthur" Sewall sent for Captain Jim. Jim heaved himself out of his rocking chair and came as always. Like Sir Harry Lauder, Jim was forever going into retirement, then bouncing out again. Didn't people realize he was getting on in years? A man of fifty-six needed to take it easy! So he began his long trip to Chile, expecting the worst, from his knowledge of Latin officials. He wasn't disappointed. He couldn't rent warehouses for the cargo.

"Senor, the sugar is spoiled by fire and water; it is worthless and only fit to jetsam. It would contaminate our beautiful clean warehouses. Yet, senor, in the interest of bettering relations between our two great nations, perhaps something can be arranged; at some expense, which is most regrettable, yet necessary."

Captain Murphy, after the usual hassle, resolved the difficulty by his direct-action methods, and returned to Bath, and "retirement" until the next time.

☆   ☆   ☆

Severe, without being brutal, quick to forgive as resent, a navigator and seaman extraordinary who was at once the wildest of sail-carriers and a cautious captain, generous to the needy, yet saving to the point of being niggardly, a sound businessman, though willing to risk his profits on a race, with a strong sense of humor, and a frightening lack of it, Captain Murphy's character was as sterling as it was contradictory.

He rounded the Horn more often than any other shipmaster. Over sixty times he made the passage which brought shipwreck and death to so many, and which at the best called up a seafarer's reserves in strength and ability. And all this without losing a life, or even a spar or sail.

Chapter Seventeen

LADYLIKE AND BRISTOL FASHION

MARY A. BROWN, beautiful, demure daughter of an English-born family, with a background as solid as Yorkshire pudding, was sixteen when she married Joshua A. Patten, of Rockland, Maine.

Joshua, already a ship's master at twenty-four, had gone to sea as a boy, studied hard and worked his way from forecastle to the quarterdeck. And on April 1, 1853, the wedding guests thought him handsome as his bride was lovely.

Mary, in her girlish happiness, little dreamed that within four years she would be hailed as one of the greatest heroines of the sea. But she was proud as Punch when her husband was given command of the new giant clipper, the 1616-ton *Neptune's Car*, two years later, in January of 1855.

Much was expected of the *Car*, and she more than came up to expectations as one of the fastest ships afloat, and the Rockland boy was the envy of master mariners everywhere.

That Joshua Patten was fitted for the task of sailing her he soon proved to the owners' satisfaction, and that he was amply fitted for the matter of handling her brawny crew, for all he was young and moreover small, there is worthy testimony. A passage that appears in the British Admiral Fitzgerald's "Memories of the Sea" evidence to this latter.

"While we were lying at Singapore we witnessed a mutiny aboard an American merchant ship," the Admiral wrote. "She was lying close to us, and was one of those splendid, well-kept clippers that were seen in all parts of the world prior to the American Civil War.

"About five o'clock one afternoon we heard a great row going on aboard the *Neptune's Car*. The crew all came aft on the quarterdeck and apparently began arguing with the three mates who were standing at the poop-rails. The altercation was obviously a very angry one. Suddenly some of the crew rushed to the fife rails, pulled out the iron belaying-pins, and let fly at the three officers who dodged as best they could.

"While this was going on something was happening that no one on board the *Neptune's Car* could see, though we could.

"A boat rowed off from shore, came under the stern of the ship, and a little man swarmed up the rope ladder hanging there. Suddenly he appeared at the break in the poop with something in his hand. He was a very small, boyish-looking fellow, but the effect of his appearance was magical. The whole crew turned and fled like a flock of sheep before a dog. They ran onto the forecastle and the little man after them. They swarmed out on the bowsprit, out onto the jibboom, where they began dropping off the end into the water like dead flies.

"One of our cutters happened to be manned alongside, and she was immediately sent away, picked up some of them and brought them aboard the *Retribution* where they were lent clothes while their own were drying, then sent on shore and handed over to the United States Consul.

"All the Yankee swank was taken out of them; they were as tame as kitten cats; when we asked them what on earth induced them to go overboard in a sharky place like Singapore, all we could get out of them was, 'That captain of ours is a snotty little cuss.' "

The 216-foot long *Neptune's Car* was placed with Patten on the California run in the trade that was booming since the discovery of gold in 1849. Everyone, it appeared, was sailing from Boston and New York to try their luck in the goldfields, and the incident referred to above occurred on the return passage of her first voyage.

When a clipper ship sailed to the West Coast, she was making a voyage of 15,000 miles or so, through gales and against head winds yet forever under pressure of making all possible speed, so that even in the worst weather she had to carry as much canvas as the captain considered barely safe.

Dangers other than from the elements were always present. They stemmed from the personnel situation. Before the Gold Rush the Yankee ships had been manned by Yankee crews, seamen all. But these too were susceptible to gold fever and were liable to vanish when the ship arrived in San Francisco, where it became necessary to fill their places for the return trip with such as were available, from waterfront scum to shanghaied foreigners.

The foreigners were generally able bodied seamen whose ability was overshadowed by resentment at their manner of being brought aboard. Of these men the "Souwegians" were long-suffering but the best; the "Limeys" inclined to stand on their rights as British subjects; while the Irishers were ready for trouble as a matter of principle.

Yet despite all this many of the captains took their wives along, so Joshua Patten, young and in love with his lovely bride, could hardly be blamed for following a custom.

That first voyage of the *Neptune's Car* was fascinating for Mary, and, it seems, uneventful apart from the Singapore incident. She found her sea legs almost before the pilot was dropped and wandered all over the ship, asking questions and making friends. She even gave Doc a hand on occasion, and as she was a good cook she was regarded as a demi-goddess both fore and aft.

Her lively manner must have impressed her husband, whose boyish manner dropped like an anchor as soon as he stepped from shore to gangplank, for he went so far as to note in the log, "Mrs. Patten is uncommon handy about the ship, even in weather, and would doubtless be of service if a man."

When Mary begged for instruction in navigation, Joshua obliged and during the balance of the 101-day passage to San Francisco she proved also to be an apt student quickly able to read a chart, plot a course or shoot the sun. By the end of the Pattens' first voyage, Mary, it was said, might easily have passed an examination for master's papers.

It was on the second voyage of the *Neptune's Car*, Captain Joshua A. Patten, that the wheel of fortune spun to bring tragedy on the one hand, and elevating Mary Patten to the annals of maritime history on the other.

It began from New York on an unusually hot day in July, 1856. The crew were all foreigners and about as hard a lot as a body could expect to clap eyes on anywhere, but strangely it was the mate, a Down Easter, who alarmed Mary. He was young, darkly handsome and swaggering and he early caused so much trouble he was suspected of being in the pay of an opposition line. The newspapers also had reported several cases where crew members, making bets on the passage of ships leaving port at the same time, for the same destination, would commit sabotage and make every effort to delay the progress of their own vessel.

With regard to the trouble on board *Neptune's Car*, a story in the NEW YORK DAILY TRIBUNE of February 18, 1857, had this to say:

"As usual with commanders in the Pacific trade, Captain Patten wished to get his ship into port ahead of his rivals. He soon found, however, that his first mate slept during half of his watch on the quarterdeck and that he kept the ship under reefed course. After repeated warnings, Captain Patten removed him."

This was quite an understatement. The mate had proved so abusive and disorderly, disregarding orders and demoralizing the crew in his attempts to delay the ship, that he was put in irons and tossed into the brig to meditate on the error of his ways. Captain Patten, instead of advancing another officer or delegating the mate's duties, took them over himself, standing two watches regularly.

As a result of this the captain held the deck day and night in approaching the Horn, refusing to go below to sleep, catching cat naps and taking his meals there. Newspapers following the voyage reported the *Car* off Cape Horn 18 days with strong westerly gales, but before the great ship pulled out of this series of storms, the captain, exhausted, had staggered to his cabin with a terrible headache and fever. Fearful that he had pneumonia, Mary dug out the ship's medical book, which was of little help for Patten had what was known as brain fever and began to suffer spells of blindness and deafness, followed by periods of complete insensibility. At other times he would rave like a madman.

Mary Patten realized she was in a grave situation, with the mate in irons and the second knowing nothing of formal navigation, fine seaman though he was. Word had already reached the crew of the captain's illness, and been passed on to Tarker, who from the brig, demanded his release and the turning over to him of the command. He pointed out that otherwise

Mary Patten would be responsible for the loss of the ship and her crew, a threat enough to frighten most women, but not Mary. She called in Mister Hare, told him she was taking over and sent a message to Tarker informing him that since the captain could not trust him when he was well, she could not trust him now that her husband was sick.

The mate's reply was to angrily advise the crew not to take orders from a female, an ugly situation which Mary quelled by calling the crew aft and telling them she could plot the course and navigate the clipper safely to San Francisco if only she could rely on them for their support. Impressed by her courage, sincerity and probably her beauty, the crew vowed loyalty in her attempt to do what no woman had ever done before: sail a tall-masted, long-sparred clipper out of the furious Cape Horn seas.

The NEW YORK DAILY TRIBUNE story continues: "Mrs. Patten, who on her previous voyage had studied navigation as a pastime, now took observations, worked up the reckoning by chronometer time, laid the ship's courses and performed the other duties of captain."

In addition to all these duties Mary succeeded in nursing her husband through the worst of his fever, and although the clipper *Intrepid* which had left port with the *Car* turned back to Rio to refit as snow, sleet and the most violent gales lashed the seas, Mary and the vessel of which she was now master carried on. She didn't have time for fear, so busy was she plotting the course, standing part of each watch and caring for Joshua. For fifty nights she did not even undress, and for one period of forty-eight hours she was on the quarterdeck, most of that time in oilskins, protected only by a weather cloth triced up to give a lee. In this blow the ship would not carry canvas and no sooner was a sail set than it was rent from clew to earing. The mizzen topsail was reduced to ribbons, and stays, shrouds and halyards parted like cotton.

Mary Patten stood the weather out, nursing the ship's head up to the seas, shouting orders by trumpet, lurching from binnacle to the companionway to consult the barometer, calculate the drift, grab an occasional cup of hot coffee, and at all opportunities seeing to Joshua.

The wind eased somewhat on the third day and with the glass rising she squared away the *Car* under a little canvas which she was prompt to increase as the weather offered. The Horn rounded, there followed, the log shows in her neat script, "a hard beat to the windward under reefed topsails and fore-topmast staysail."

As the ship sped northward, Captain Patten partially recovered from his fever. Still too weak for mental and physical exertion he decided to release the mate, a decision which Tarker repaid with advances to Mary. What actually happened was never made clear. The watch reported hearing Mary's excited cries and when they came running were told there had been a "dreadful accident." Evidently there had, for Tarker was lying across the doorway to her cabin, a large lump on his forehead. When she next discovered that he had altered course for Valparaiso the captain had her call the four mates and entire crew aft, at which time it was announced the first mate was demoted to forecastle hand and under arrest again.

At this Mister Hare was promoted to Tarker's place and the captain, after giving orders that the ship was to be taken to no port but San Francisco, had a relapse and for the next 25 days was totally blind again.

Among her many burdens Mary had another which she hoped was secret, yet was not. She was in the advanced stages of pregnancy. She did not allow this to interfere with her duties as the *Car* beat its way up the 2,500-mile coast to Chile to warmer waters. Canvas was crowded on and the big ship logged over three hundred miles in one day, but with San Francisco less than a week away they ran out of winds. This was a doubly dangerous blow to Mary. Her baby was due at any time, but it was Joshua who was causing her the greatest concern, for any further delay in receiving medical treatment could be a matter of life and death to him.

It was ten more wearisome days before a light breeze sprang up and the vessel limped into port, an entry in the log by Mary noting the voyage had taken 136 days. In San Francisco, after meeting with the agent and consignee and turning over the manifest, Mary repaired to the Oriental Hotel where she was besieged by reporters. Her tale had every ingredient dreamed of to make readers and writers happy, and the newspapers helped raise a fund which made it possible for the Pattens to return to Boston on the steamship *George Law*. The underwriters sent her a gift of $1,000, together with a letter which said in part:

"We know of no instance where the love and devotion of a wife have been more impressively portrayed than in your watchfulness and care of your husband during his long, painful illness. Nor do we know of an instance on record where a woman has been called upon to assume command of a large and valuable vessel, and exercised a proper control over a large number of seamen, and by her own skill and energy impressing them with a confidence and reliance making all subordinate, and obedient to that command."

So critical was Joshua's condition that the Pattens stayed for two weeks in New York before moving on to Boston. By now Mary realized he would never recover, but for his sake forced a cheerfulness she did not feel. In both cities she was lauded by the press; in fact the story had become international and she was urged to join the Woman's Rights movement and to make lecture tours, but she was now too weary and worried to take interest in such matters.

On March 10, 1857, she gave birth to a son, Joshua Adams Patten, but it is doubtful if the captain ever knew he was a father for he died, still unconscious, July 25, in a hospital at Somerville, Massachusetts. The city observed a period of mourning and church bells tolled and harbor shipping lowered their ensigns to half-mast.

A fund of $1,400 was raised for Mary and her child, but the strength and determination that had been her mainstay for so long seemed to have vanished with her husband's death. She contracted typhoid, then tuberculosis, and before her son was four years old joined her husband in Woodlawn Cemetery, Everett, Massachusetts. The Pattens were finally home from the sea.

Young Joshua was taken by his grandparents to their home in Rockland and the hospital at Kings Point Academy, New York, was named after his mother, the greatest and probably the most courageous of the Blue Water Women.

Chapter Eighteen

FATHER OF THE NAVY

Edward Preble was born in 1761, when Portland was still the Town of Falmouth, District of Maine, Province of Massachusetts. The town's face was to the sea and sailors were to be seen everywhere; on the waterfront and even on streets in the quieter sections. Tall-masted ships crowded the harbor and cargoes were carried out to and brought back from the West Indies, Old England, Bombay and the ports of China. No growing boy could help but take an interest in such exciting scenes, and young Ed was no exception.

His father, Brigadier Jedediah Preble, was a redoubtable figure in the history and economy of the colonial era. An active man of imposing stature, he was said to have been the first, white or red, to climb Mt. Washington. Big in every sense of the word, a political leader with considerable wealth and far-flung enterprises, he was not a "stuffed shirt" like so many of the colonial hierachy. A member of the Church of England, his household was therefore less straightlaced than those of his neighbors, all Congregationalists, the leading church after the Puritan takeover. With twelve children and an easy-going father, it was a lively and noisy place indeed. The Brigadier himself was always roaring with laughter, for he was a great hand with practical jokes. None, regardless of station in life, was safe from his outrageous humor, nor did his children escape.

Edward was the especial butt for his humor, but the tricks played on him usually backfired. Even at ten he had an uncanny knack for turning the tables.

Two of his father's jokes are remembered. One began with the arrival of a vessel from the East, with a fierce-looking Turk in the crew, his appearance accentuated by ferocious whiskers. Edward, intrigued by this individual, made inquiries concerning him to his father, who gleefully made the most of the occasion. The sailor was the son of "Black Mahound," the most fiendish

villain in the world, who made a habit of carrying off little boys
to his own land, for purposes too horrible to be even guessed at,
the elder Preble explained seriously.   Edward was impressed
and very thoughtful.

That evening the wily Brigadier arranged it so that Edward
and one of his younger brothers would be left alone in the house,
the only light from the logs burning in the fireplace.   A noise at
the window brought them to instant attention.   It was the Terrible Turk, climbing through the window with a leather bag in
his hand, in which to stuff little boys.   The Brigadier, watching
from the outside through another window, nudged a friend.
"This will be good," he said.

The little brother stood frozen, but Edward didn't panic the
least bit.   He grabbed a burning brand from the hearth and
thrust it into the Turk's scowling face, and the Terrible One
went back out of the window screaming, whiskers ablaze.

"That boy doesn't scare easy," the Brigadier admitted
proudly, if ruefully.

☆   ☆   ☆

On another occasion the Brigadier set out with some friends
to row to one of the nearer offshore islands.   The boy wanted
to go along, but the small boat was already crowded.   And anyway, the Brigadier wanted to see how his precocious son would
take being left behind.

He found out promptly enough.   Enraged by the refusal,
Edward, who all his life was a proponent of direct action, took
it now.   He followed the boat along the shore, pelting its occu-
pants with stones and his aim was true. When his father headed
the boat into shore, his guests eagerly awaited the thrashing
that he would deservedly give his unruly offspring.   They were
shocked when laughing heartily, he took the boy aboard, remarking that "he'll be a general some day."

Not much more is known of Edward's boyhood.   Sent to
Dummer Academy, his chief interest there was in outdoor
sports.   He seldom attained more than fair grades, except in
two studies, speaking and writing, subjects in which he would
excel in maturity.

With a prankster for a father and the turmoil of a large
family made unruly by the head of it, where then did Edward
acquire his strong sense of discipline; of himself and others,

that became so marked in his later life? And if he inherited any of his parent's humor, it was in the form of a ready wit that could at times be sharp to the point of unpleasantness.

When Falmouth (now Portland) was bombarded and burned in 1775 by Mowatt, the Preble family like so many others, came down from easy affluence to bare subsistence level. Edward was brought home from school to help his brothers on the family farm, a life he despised. He stood it for one season, but with the war and lurid accounts of sea battles and adventure on the high seas to be heard everywhere in the town, he began to ponder the situation. Sent back to school again, when the school year of 1776-77 came to a close, with only the prospect of grubbing in the soil ahead for the summer, he took off for Newburyport, a center of privateer activity, and there signed on as cabin boy aboard the *Neptune*, twenty-four guns, Captain William Friend.

The Brigadier, when he heard the news, instead of exploding into fury, took the escapade in his stride. "Let the runaway go," he said. "One voyage aboard a privateer will cure him of any notion of making the sea his profession." He couldn't have been more wrong.

Edward was as bored with life as cabin boy as he had been with farming, so he spent as much time as possible on the deck or in running about the rigging like an over-sized monkey. He learned rapidly, especially as Captain Friend was indulgent and even went so far as to change the articles to give the boy ordinary seaman status. At the end of the cruise a blank space develops in the recorded career of Edward Preble, and we next hear of him receiving a midshipman's warrant aboard the new Massachusetts State ship *Protector*, commissioned during the winter of 1779.

The *Protector* of the State Navy was a cross between a light frigate and heavy corvette, an unhandy size for any man-of-war. The fact that she carried twenty-six guns didn't help her sailing qualities any. After one brief and unsatisfactory cruise, the Massachusetts Congress sent her to the Grank Banks, to stand on and off in the track of the rich merchantmen bound from the West Indies for London and Europe.

It was on the morning of June 9, 1780, that the fog lifted to show, according to the log, a "large ship to the windward under

English colors, standing down before the wind for us, we being to the leeward.   Looked as large as a 74; by the set of her yards, not a warship, yet she seemed willing enough for action ... ''

The Royal Navy didn't think too well of American fighting ability in the Revolution, and merchantmen were as quick to close as a man-of-war, often to their sorrow.   But while from the British point of view the Americans weren't much on the sea, they did offer just enough fighting to keep the well-disciplined Royal Navy crews in trim.

The "Lobsterbacks" must have been rather disconcerted when the awkward sailing *Protector,* instead of running for it, stood on under sail, and the bosun piped all hands to quarters. The Britisher hove-to then, under fighting canvas of jibs and topsails, ports triced up and guns run out, but as yet not a shot was fired.

Protector came down with the bone in her teeth, luffed under the enemy lee quarter and let go a broadside.   The British responded with three cheers and a broadside of their own.   Then both vessels ran down a reach with the wind abeam, each firing a gun every few minutes at close range, making an almighty big noise, but few hits, for both vessels were amateurs at war. The British were at a disadvantage; the sides of their ship were so high that it was difficult to bring guns to bear.   With the thick, rolling clouds of yellow-white smoke the gunners failed to notice this fact and kept right on shooting over the American's tops.

The marines in these tops, unlike the American seamen, were not amateurs at fighting; they were backwoods marksmen, many former rangers, and they cleared the enemy tops in jigtime.   Then they turned their attention to the decks and gun crews.   After an hour the British helmsman was killed and before he could be replaced, the big ship fell off, her bowsprit crashing over *Protector's* quarter.

The Americans lashed it fast and boarders were called away, the seamen crowding aft, the marines firing into the British ports.   But before the boarders could mount, a huge swell broke the lashings and as the merchantman swung, *Protector* fired a steady raking broadside which brought down the mizzenmast and set the main topgallant afire.   The blaze ran down the rigging and the marines shot down every Englishman who tried to fight it. Sparks dropped in a hogshead of paper cartridges and the resulting explosion blew off the quarterdeck. The enemy ship began to sink rapidly by the stern and her people leaped overboard to escape the spreading flames. *Protector's* boats were got away and managed to save fifty-five of the enemy, at least half of them wounded.

The lost ship turned out to be the *Admiral Duff*, thirty-six guns, a West India letter-of-marque London-bound with sugar and tobacco. Sight of the American had intensified a desire for "easy pickings," for it was well-known that Yankees wouldn't fight. Now the British sheepishly admitted that they had never before run into such deadly marksmanship.

Oddly enough, no mention is made of the part Midshipman Preble played in this, his first naval engagement, in the reports, official or otherwise. The fact remains that he "was there," and if the history that was yet to be written is any indication, he was in the thick of it. It is known, however, that he had command of a division of main-deck guns. He must have done well with them, for at the age of nineteen he was promoted to a lieutenancy.

The *Duff* had carried fever aboard and sixty Americans came down with it. Short-handed, the Massachusetts ship was lucky to escape H.M.S. *Thames*, 32 guns, after a running fight. Laid up for refitting and recruiting, she then set out on a West Indies cruise and captured several prizes. In May of 1781, she fell in with two British frigates, one of her own class, the other of fifty guns. Out-sailed, out-gunned and out-maneuvered, she was easily taken.

Mr. Lieutenant Preble was now a prisoner of war and therefore in the power of British Provost Marshal Cunningham and his Commissary side-kick, Loring. When he stood on his legal rights as a prisoner of war and refused to get up the money that might have eased his situation, or send to his father for it, he was tossed into the most horrible of all the prison hulks, the *Jersey*, in New York harbor. Few escaped alive from this vermin and fever-ridden trap. If they didn't die of disease, they wasted away from malnutrition, for Cunningham sold their wretched food supplies whenever he had the opportunity.

Young Edward contracted a fever that was probably typhus, and without doubt would have ended up among the corpses that went over the side daily to the waiting burial barges, had it not been for a lucky break.

This stroke of luck came in the form of a British officer of a Loyal American regiment, who came aboard on a tour of inspection. He was Colonel Tyng, a former Falmouth (Portland) resident and a friend of the family who had served with the Brigadier in the Old French War. An important man and long-time sheriff, he had been forced to flee the town at the outbreak of hostilities due to his Tory leanings. Now he proved a real friend. He nursed Edward through the worst of his illness, saw that he had proper nourishment and arranged his exchange, for which the United States Navy and the people of this nation should be forever grateful. Although a political enemy, he did not forget that he was a friend and an American.

It took young Edward a full year of outdoor living in the health-giving air of Maine to restore him sufficiently so that he might again go to sea. While he was waiting he studied every book he could find on his chosen profession. By the time he reached the ripe old age of twenty-one, he had earned a reputation for capability in command, as well as for sudden bursts of temper, which luckily "did not last long enough for him to take a turn of the quarterdeck."

As First Lieutenant of the Massachusetts ship *Winthrop*, newly commissioned, Captain George Little, his responsibility was great. He felt, with reason, that his was a marvelous opportunity to serve under such an expert seaman.

The *Winthrop* was sloop-rigged. Not as a sloop-of-war, which could be anything, including a full-rigged ship, but an actual one-sticker, though large. She carried but twelve guns, yet conducted one of the best minor cruises of the War, operating off the Maine coast through the summer of 1782. She captured two large privateers and a vessel of unspecified class, but it was only the beginning.

Toward the end of August Captain Little learned that the British brig *Allegiance*, 14 guns, was out to get *Winthrop*. With Castine as a base and lying over each night under protection of the fort's guns, she was searching high and low for the Yankee sloop, without taking any chances.

Little decided to find the enemy before the brig found him; to cut her out in a night raid. Forty men, the bulk of his command, dressed in white smocks for identification, were told off with Lieutenant Preble in charge. The sloop slid into Castine harbor under cover of darkness and laid alongside the brig without discovery. Preble leaped into the brig's main-chains with fourteen of his forty behind him, then the *Winthrop*, which evidently had too much way, came loose and the vessels drifted apart, leaving Preble and his fourteen to handle the entire British crew.

"Do you need more men?" Little called worriedly.

"No," Preble bellowed back, in a voice that rose above the roar of battle, the pistol shots, the clanging cutlasses, the cursing. "We have too many now; they stand in each others' way."

Suddenly the British panicked and broke. Some leaped overboard, others surrendered. Leaving the prisoners under guard, Preble with a few men burst into the cabin. "Resistance is useless," he told the startled officers, who were just beginning to turn out. Then he got way on his prize and sailed her past the fort before that stronghold came to life. The "cutting out" had been a bold and skillful performance and the best part of all, he had not lost a man. That is the way to fight a war, Preble mused in satisfaction. Keep it one-sided.

The sloop took several more prizes. Yet despite the fact that she was successful, she was sold out of service, for Massachusetts had grown weary of maintaining a navy. Let the Continental Congress have that chore. So Edward Preble, through no fault of his own, was on the beach, but not for long. He had made a reputation and his family was influential. He was appointed our resident commercial agent in Spain. For the next fifteen years his was a busy life, but not in a military sense. A voyage to the West Indies; to Bordeaux in command of a ship; a trading voyage to New Guinea as master of the brig *Polly*. This last venture turned into a failure when he refused to ship a return cargo of slaves.

Back home in Maine part of the time, on one occasion the violence of his nature, so carefully guarded, exploded into action. A public document advises all men that "whereas Edward Preble in the city of Cumberland in the month of March dealt James Lamb a violent blow in the head with a gun, the said Preble has

given the said Lamb $245 and received a quit-claim." Is it any
wonder that Edward Preble grew more and more cold in his attitude toward humanity? The frozen exterior was a safety
measure for its protection.

On another of his voyages his vessel was intercepted by a
French cruiser, taken into port and condemned as a prize and
Preble was placed under house arrest on the grounds that he
was violating American neutrality by carrying merchandise of
British origin. This was becoming a regular French pattern
of behavior and one that didn't set well with Americans. So
President Adams went before the Congress and asked for authority to complete the three big frigates that had been laid
down four years past, when the Barbary pirates were acting up.
The construction of these vessels had been abandoned when the
cutthroats condescended to accept tribute instead of roundshot.

To make certain that the Navy had force, some smaller warships were authorized as well, and to the six captains on the list,
lieutenants were added, and Preble was one.

☆   ☆   ☆

Mr. Stephen Higginson of Boston, local Navy agent for the
Federal Government, was worried, although from his demeanor
one would never suspect it. For not only was he a Yankee, but
a Boston Brahmin to boot, and it would never do to let lesser
folk discover that he was human. Nonetheless, in his report
which on Wednesday, June 6, 1798, he sat down to write, he was
slightly indiscreet. In black and white was his blunt statement
that regardless of all the President's appointments to the new
frigate *Constitution,* now in preparation for sea, as his, Mr.
Higginson's responsibility, but one officer was fit for command;
namely, Mr. Edward Preble. He goes on to list the many dis-
qualifications of the others and concludes, "Mr. Preble, the first
Lt is a smart active popular man, judicious & well qualified for
his station, or for the first command." As a postscript, Mr. Higginson thought the new First Lieutenant would refuse to go in
the *Constitution* once he made the acquaintance of his fellow
officers. The Navy agent was right.

The frigate was now lying at Mr. Hartt's wharf, lower
shrouds ratted down as workmen hove on ropes to sway up the
topmasts. Mr. Higginson, a highly patriotic gentlemen, had

contributed three thousand dollars from his own pocket and two thousand in the name of his son toward her building, and he was determined that the big frigate of forty-four guns would go out properly found and geared. For fifteen years the Navy had possessed no warships, a national disgrace to his mind, as it was to all good Federalists. He hadn't quite approved of the design at first. It was new, therefore untried, but she had turned out first-rate. She had the planking of a battleship to begin with, and taller spars than ever before placed on a vessel of her class.

Of course, in the taverns, it was frequently pointed out that money spent on her was wasted, for she was doomed. Godfrey, hadn't she stuck on the ways at her launching, and had to be prodded into the water, weeks after the guests of honor had gone home? It was all superstitious nonsense and did not bother Mr. Higginson in the least, as a rational man, or he had been before President Adams' proclamation had arrived, authorizing all public ships of the United States to take and bring into port armed vessels "acting under the authority or pretense of authority of the French Republic."

Hailed with glee in Boston of all places, the people sang in the streets and the theatres,
"Immortal patriots, rise once more!
Defend your homes, defend your shore!"
It meant war for sure and Mr. Higginson couldn't bear the thought of his beautiful new frigate in Davy Jones' Locker, where she would be unless properly officered. Worse still, her captain, one Samuel Nickerson, was a foreigner from a place called Maryland. Only a Yankee should captain a Yankee ship. Anybody with a grain of sense would know that, but did the Secretary of the Navy have any? Minded to give him some, Mr. Higginson again sat down at his table and took pen in hand.

Thirty-six at this time, Edward Preble was a tall man with heavy, powerful shoulders and a commanding presence. His lips were tight in a long face, topped by red hair that curled thickly around a balding forehead. He had a nervous energy and was quick in all his movements; was in fact, seldom quiet when awake. A great hunter like his father, he was also an athlete who could outdo younger men in any contest. He was socially popular, had traveled widely and dealt with people on the highest political and social levels. His manners held a genuine courtliness, enhanced by the best traditions of his New England background.

Preble remained in Boston when the *Constitution* sailed in July of 1798. When the revenue cutter *Pickering* was taken into the naval service, he was given her command, with the advanced rank of Lieutenant-Commandant. A brig of fourteen guns and seventy men, she spent the next six months cruising West India waters and also did convoy duty down and back. The British, delighted by an unexpected ally, made their ports available to American vessels. On the whole it was uneventful service, though the brig did recapture a former prize, a near wreck with her foremast down. When he examined her papers he discovered that she had been under command of his brother Joseph, now a prisoner of the "Frogs."

The log books of the brig give indication of the readiness with which Preble kept her for action. One entry is repeated over and over. "Gave chase. Beat to quarters. Furnished the men in the tops with a pair of pistols and sharpened cutlass apiece." This was an innovation. Only marines had been armed in the tops. In a new navy, Preble felt he had a right to set a precedent.

His squadron commander was John Barry. Returning home before the Portlander and his little brig, the Commodore's report stated flatly that Preble was one of the ablest officers in the service. He added that he sincerely hoped Preble would not resign; a possibility he had often spoken of. Preble was not well; had long been troubled with stomach ulcers. Furthermore, he had an agreement with his commercial firm that after one naval cruise he would return to the merchant service.

All this was known to Authority and on the basis of Barry's report a letter was waiting for Preble when he arrived in New York in June of 1799. It was from the newly appointed Secretary of the Navy, Benjamin Stoddert, and read: "President Adams has been pleased to promote Lieutenant Preble to the grade of Captain, to take effect immediately, and will give him a good ship if he remains in the service. For the present, Captain Preble is to repair to Boston and await orders."

It was a tempting offer and Preble went up to Boston and hung around waiting for orders that didn't come. His time wasn't wasted for he completed his shoreside work for the commercial firm and studied every book available pertaining to naval warfare. Then, in October, the orders came. He was to take over the new frigate *Essex*, 32 guns, now at Salem, a gift of that town to the United States. She was to proceed to the East Indies in company with the frigate *Congress*, 38, taking down a small convoy and returning with a big one, valued conservatively at several million dollars.

The captain of the *Congress* was senior officer, and therefore commodore. Less than three days out the warships ran into a warm Gulf Stream gale. Riggings set up in a New England winter now went slack and the bracings no longer held the spars in place. *Congress* pitched all three masts and limped into port jury-rigged. Preble, a better seaman than his associate, had taken advance measures, saved his command from rigging trouble and pushed on with the convoy. In the process, the Stars and Stripes were carried east of Good Hope for the first time.

Otherwise it was an uneventful cruise. Long ago Preble had learned how to keep men healthy on an extended voyage. He returned to port with but nine men on the sick list, all with tropical fevers, a record for a navy of the day. The Secretary advised all other captains to study Preble's methods. Only drawback to this record was that Preble himself was one of the nine. Hardly had he brought the ship into home port when the fever, of a nature from which he was never fully to recover, grew worse.

While he was convalescing, orders came from Washington to fit *Essex* for sea again, as part of a squadron of three sailing to give the Barbary pirates their come-uppance. Truxton, that fabulous hero, was in command.

Despite his poor health, Preble insisted on carrying out his orders, but by the time the frigate was ready to sail, sickness forced him to request leave. It was granted and he promptly bought a house in Norfolk, married a Maine heiress named Margaret Deering, and settled down to combine a honeymoon with his recovery.

Meanwhile, Truxton, that doughty fighter of the French War, knew his rights and was sensitive to the least slight. A commodore should not sail his own ship; he should have a flag captain, and by chowder, he Truxton, would have one. To the men in power, this attitude smacked of aristocratic leanings, not suitable for a republic's navy. His request was curtly refused and Truxton immediately resigned.

He was replaced by Richard Dale, an old man who had been a lieutenant under John Paul Jones. Dale took the squadron to the Mediterranean and set up a partial blockade of Tripoli, the leading miscreant state. Little was accomplished.

A year later Captain Richard V. Morris took out a squadron of three heavy frigates and two light ones. One vessel was badly damaged by an explosion and he handled the others so poorly that the pirates "had it made" for the rest of the summer, chasing American merchantmen in all directions and forcing prisoners into slave labor. The Navy Department ordered Morris home, and after a Board of Inquiry, dismissed him from the service.

This seemed unduly harsh, for his only crime was error in judgment. Yet something was decidedly wrong with our naval establishment, and just what was a matter for conjecture. It was generally agreed, however, that shock treatment was needed, so poor Morris was thrown to the wolves.

The fact that the Navy had been reduced to a peace footing didn't help the situation. Officers had been let go in wholesale lots, salaries had been cut, and there was no longer prospect of prize-money. Morale was at an all-time low. Only nine captains were retained, and Edward Preble of Portland was one. Even he had tried to resign.

John Barry was the senior captain still in the service. Preble stood sixth. In 1803, Secretary of the Navy Smith, who never for the rest of his life did anything else of such importance, appointed the Mainer to command in the Mediterranean. It was not done with thought of improving the service, but because Preble was known to be a good officer and the logical choice. Few in power, from President Jefferson on down, realized that the stern Portlander could develop his qualities of leadership to a degree that would make him father of our modern navy.

Preble's squadron would consist of the frigate *Constitution*, 44, a second heavy frigate, *Philadelphia*, 38, three schooners, *Enterprise*, 12, *Nautilus*, 12, and *Vixen*, 12. Two brigs, *Argus* and *Siren*, both 16's, were like the last two schooners, brand new. These light vessels were needed to work inshore on the North African coast, with its many reefs. And it was only by their use that the blockade could be enforced against the small pirate craft; the coasters of felucca rig, used by the Tripolitans to bring in grains and other food supplies.

Preble was in personal command of *Constitution*. Unlike his predecessors, he had informed himself in detail respecting the enemy; his forces, personnel, way of life and sources of supplies. He knew the location of every gun in the pirate forts, the exact number of white renegades that captained them, and even the exact number of women in the harem of Peter Lisle, the red-haired Scot who was admiral of the pirate navy. Evidently Preble had a large and efficient secret service. In this work he was assisted by the British and Danes, "neutrals" in the semi-war, as their governments had paid the tribute demanded by the Bashaw.

It rapidly became evident that Preble was thinking of more than blockade. Like his father before him, he was a believer in direct action. One of his first reports to the Secretary of the Navy asks for mortar ships (only necessary in bombardment of fortifications). They can be bought in Italy, he says. He also wants authority to purchase the same type of light craft used by the pirates.

His plan was not to act as a super-policeman; to prevent the pirates from attacking and taking American shipping. His plan was to sink their misbegotten navy, go in and blow the forts to Kingdom Come, land and completely wipe out the nest of vipers for all time. In the process, of course, he would have the extreme pleasure of hanging the renegades, starting with Lisle, for without their know-how the pirate effort would not have amounted to much. It was a policy that set well with the personnel of his squadron; especially the young lieutenants and midshipmen. Here, they said gleefully, is a real fighting commander, in the time-honored American tradition. Maybe the Navy wouldn't be so bad after all for a career.

They were all very young, those officers, and when Preble first met them, he blew his top. "Why, they are nothing but a pack of boys," he raged. The officer nearest his own age, Bainbridge, was twenty years his junior. To make matters worse, they were nearly all southerners. How could any self-respecting Yankee hope to get along with such men, who were as ready to duel as take a drink, excitable as they were adventurous? Preble, formal and precise, was considered something of a tyrant by these youngsters, at first, but if the tyrant would fight as his plans indicated, he was acceptable to them.

Aboard the flagship *Constitution,* the atmosphere on the way out had been strained to put it mildly — until the incident of the "midnight encounter."

The frigate was close under Gibraltar. A huge bulk loomed out of the dark, running parallel to the American. In the heaving seaway, the stranger looked like a "liner."

Both vessels hailed together and both refused to give suitable answer. In the confusion of shouts, each commander tried to discover the identity of the other vessel, without revealing his own. Preble could keep his unruly temper under control only up to a point. That point was long past. He grabbed a speaking trumpet from the officer of the deck. "I now hail you for the last time," he roared. "If you do not answer me, I'll fire a shot into you."

"If you fire a shot, I'll return a broadside," the reply came down from high in the darkness. It must be a thundering big ship. The boy officers held their breath.

"I should like to see you try that," Preble suggested. "I now hail you for an answer. What ship is that?"

"This is H.M.S. *Donegal,* 84, Sir Richard Strachan, an English commodore. Send a boat aboard."

"This is the U.S.S. *Constitution,*" Preble shouted. "44 guns, Edward Preble, an American commodore. I'll be damned if I'll send a boat aboard any ship." Preble, from his precarious perch on the hammocks and holding hard to a stay, leaned back to call down to the gun captains, loud enough for everybody aboard the other ship to hear, "Blow on your matches, boys!"

It was the Englishman who sent a boat, and the *Donegal,* instead of a ship-of-the-line, proved to be a 32-ton frigate.

Preble hadn't known that the Britisher was bluffing, and his junior officers were delighted. What an Old Man they had! Why, he was ready to take the *Constitution* into battle in the darkness, against an opponent three times her force. This commodore evidently had the right stuff in him, even if he was a Maine Puritan. So he was a tyrant and hard as nails, but it was worth taking a dressing down on occasion to serve under such a rip-snorting fighter.

Many years later, those young officers who were still alive reached an important conclusion. The Britisher had not reacted out of fear, but from the surprising awareness that an American frigate was ready for action while the talking was going on, the matches burning and the cartridges laid out, the powder monkeys sanding the deck.

Thus Edward Preble, always ready for action or talk, set an example that was not wasted on the young men who served under him.

At Gibraltar, Preble found orders to shift the American base from the "Rock" to Malta. This would extend his line of communications. If Morocco, holder of a key position in the Straits, declared war, this line would be cut. Advised that a state of unofficial war already existed (the Moors had just taken an American brig, recaptured by Bainbridge in the *Philadelphia*), Spanish sources said that another American had been taken, the crew now in a dungeon. Preble was annoyed. "This state of affairs will never do." He gave orders to take all Moorish vessels. Then after setting up the blockade of Tripoli, he sailed his remaining three frigates and a Moorish prize into Tangier harbor, ports triced up and cleared for action.

Going ashore, Preble paid a courtesy call on His Majesty, the Emperor of Morocco, who obviously didn't care for Yankees. He asked the Mainer if he wasn't worried about being detained. "Not at all," Preble said largely, waving his hand in direction of the harbor and the American squadron, with every gun apparently aimed directly at the palace. "If I fail to return at the expected time, my squadron will lay your batteries, your castle and your city in ruins in an hour."

"There must be a mistake somewhere," the Emperor admitted. "I've always been friendly to your government; to Americans in general." To prove it, the Moorish miscreant released his American prisoners. For this generous gesture, Preble returned the 22-gun captured warship.

That was Preble diplomacy, usually successful, for he believed that it was only possible to negotiate from a position of strength.

En route to Malta, he was spoken by the British frigate *Amazon*, with the shocking news that the great *Philadelphia* had been taken by the Tripolitans, though no one was to blame for what happened on October 31, 1803, least of all Bainbridge. It was simply an accident. *Vixen* had been there to prevent just such a mishap, but the schooner had been sent to the west'ard on a chase, while the frigate took off after another that ran close to Tripoli harbor and inshore. As the big frigate came about, the wind and tide were right to drive her on an uncharted reef.

Bainbridge and his people did everything possible to get her off; hauled the guns aft, braced the yards aback, cut away the anchors and finally hove most of the iron. Even the foremast was cut away. It was no use. The pirate gunboats swarmed around, firing steadily. The frigate was canted so badly that none of her remaining pieces would bear. Bainbridge gave up. He had holes bored in the frigate's bottom and hauled down the flag. It was a real disaster for American prospects, but worse was to come. Two days later a strong northerly piled so much water over the reef that the frigate floated free. The enemy quickly patched her holes and towed her into Tripoli harbor. Now they had a warship to match the infidel's great *Constitution*.

The officers and crew of the *Philadelphia* were of immense diplomatic and financial value as prisoners, and the Bashaw gleefully sent word to Preble that as a preliminary to further negotiations, he would take one thousand dollars a head for the unfortunates, adding that if the money was not forthcoming, said heads would roll.

Was the villain bluffing? His past reputation was bloodthirsty enough. Preble knew that something had to be done — quickly. And the *Philadelphia* must be destroyed before she could be repaired and used against the Americans. This was also the idea held by Bainbridge, who communicated with Preble through cipher and the good offices of the Danish consul.

Preble sailed *Constitution* down to Tripoli to study the situation at close range, then ran back to his new base at Syracuse, where the flag was shifted to *Vixen*, as he did not want to risk damage to the frigate from winter gales. With his small vessels he maintained a stiff blockade through one of the most severe Mediterranean winters on record.

Lieutenant Stephen Decatur, in command of the fast-sailing lucky little schooner *Enterprise*, 12, who was close to the Commodore, was probably first to hear of the project against *Philadelphia*. They worked the details out together, which closely followed those of the cutting-out expedition against *Allegiance* at Castine in the old war of Preble's youth.

The success of the undertaking would be surprise. A ketch, recently captured from the pirates, would be just the ticket, as she would not be recognized for an American. Renamed *Intrepid* and filled with seventy-four eager volunteers, with Decatur in command, she made a night raid into the harbor. *Philadelphia* was boarded, burned and blown up, an astounding story in itself, and a great load was taken off Preble's mind. Now he could get to work.

His nature was as eager and active as Decatur's. He planned a new and large-scale attack and wrote about it to Washington. He will borrow light-draft gunboats and mortar craft from the King of the Two Sicilies, he says. He needs one hundred barrels of powder at once, "for I intend to blow up the Bashaw's works." And while he was on the subject, there was another closely related project, a scheme that stemmed from the busy mind of William Eaton, American consul at Tunis.

The Bashaw had a brother; one that he had carelessly neglected to murder. Hamet was his name and he claimed to be the rightful ruler of Tripoli. Both Eaton and Preble were certain that the present American squadron had force enough to place Hamet in power over the secondary cities of Derna and Benghazi. This would place an enemy in the Bashaw's rear.

Six gunboats and two mortar vessels came with the spring. All were in poor repair, but quickly put in commission. The reinforcements did not come, but Preble determined to attack without them. "Having no vessel in the Squadron excepting this ship *Constitution*, whose cannon can make any Impression on the Bashaw's walls, I expect we may suffer much." It was a possibility that didn't bother him overmuch, nor did he in the waiting period slacken his iron discipline.

In late July of 1804 the squadron sailed, and on the 28th was before Tripoli. Mortars threw shells into the town, but action was broken off because of a freshening offshore wind that made it dangerous to remain. On August 3rd the blow died down and the squadron once more moved in to attack.

Tripoli harbor is formed by a long tongue of land, and from it a line of reefs and shoals extend eastward. The town, on which were the main defenses, stood behind the spit. A big castle-fort named English rose on the southeast shore. The enemy had sixteen lateen-rigged gunboats, each with a heavy and light gun, in readiness to operate between the reefs, as they had done during the capture of *Philadelphia*.

Preble moved in with *Constitution* until he was within point-blank range of the Castle, his lighter vessels lined behind. The mortars fired over the batteries into the town and the borrowed gunboats surged up from the tail of his column and locked with enemy craft in fierce combat; hand-to-hand, a form of fighting for which the pirates prided themselves.

Decatur led the light craft with the expectation that here would be the hottest fighting. He was not disappointed. When the action was over he mounted to *Constitution's* deck, handsome face streaked with blood and black with powder, though the grime could not cover the sadness brought about by the mortal wounding of his brother. "Sir," he reported with weary pride, "I have brought you three of the enemy's gunboats."

Preble in a sudden rage, seized Decatur by the lapels of his short boarding jacket. Almost shaking his favorite officer, he roared, "Only three, sir? Where are the rest of them? Why have you not brought me more, sir?"

Decatur stiffened and wrenched away. His face reddened, then paled. He clapped a hand to his belt where he usually wore a dirk. Luckily it wasn't there. The other officers stared dumbly, in transfixed horror.

The Commodore disdainfully turned his back and stalked away. Two long minutes passed, while Decatur stood motionless. The silence grew unbearable. Suddenly a messenger appeared. "The Commodore's compliments, sir, and would Captain Decatur be good enough to repair to the cabin?"

Captain Decatur would, and did, and for a long time the officers on deck waited, fearing the worst and expecting it. The
silence grew and deepened, broken only by the wash of water
along the hull, the wind whispering through the rigging, and the
other small sounds of a working ship. Finally one of the younger lieutenants could stand the tension no longer. Walking soft-
ly, he dropped down the companionway ladder and along the
passage to the Commodore's cabin. He stood with bated breath,
listening for some indication of violence within. Gathering his
courage he tapped on the door, then flung it open.

The stern Commodore from Maine and his brave but excitable young captain were seated side by side on a cabin bench —
and both men were in tears!

The captured gunboats were refitted and on the 7th Preble
renewed the assault, the American vessels crowding the fort at
the base of the spit, the fast schooners standing off the pirate
gunboats. The wind was offshore, so *Constitution* kept wearing
room and gave distant support. The light craft took a beating
and one gunboat blew up, losing half her crew. Yet the sea-
battery walls were destroyed, many of the guns dismounted and
any number of pirates killed, added to considerable damage to
the town.

The Bashaw made peace overtures. Why all the useless
bloodshed, he asked? To show his own peaceful intent he was
even willing to forego all tribute in the future and cut the ran-
som for the prisoners he held; those poor unfortunate Americans, taken while doing their duty and now languishing in
chains. Such suffering was so unnecessary. All Preble had to
do (the infidel dog) was hoist anchor and go away.

Although the gentle Bashaw was breaking his heart,
Preble's reply to this generous offer was that he would not pay
a red cent. If harm came to the prisoners, so much the worse
for the Bashaw, who would be held personally responsible. He
towed his mortars into position for a night bombardment. It
was not a success, for both the weapons and powder were of in-
ferior manufacture.

Preble tried a new trick. At three a.m. the gunboats were
sent to close the gaps in the reef. They anchored and began

firing at the pirate shipping and the town. In the semi-dark-
ness of early dawn the pirates could not find points to aim at for
effective reply, as the closed gaps made the reefs look like one
stretch of jagged rock.

This time the American bombardment was more than satisfactory. People were seen running into the fields and the desert
beyond, and a big ketch was sunk at her moorings. The pirate
gunboats entered the fight. Three were shot to kindling. Then
with daybreak, *Constitution* came gliding in to musket-shot
range, blowing open the shore batteries and covering withdrawal
of the light vessels.

The Americans worked at destruction eighteen hours a
day. On September 3rd the entire squadron moved in, the
Constitution taking on the town and castle alone, twenty-six
broadside guns against seventy. She was so close to the enemy
and fired so rapidly, that her gunnery formed her own cover.

After this great bombardment the weather turned foul, but
Edward Preble and his squadron had taught the pirates a lesson
to remember. The long awaited reinforcements arrived under
Captain Samuel Barron, who ranked the Mainer and therefore
took command of the combined fleet. Tobias Lear, that un-
savory character with the rank of "Political Officer" now under-
took negotiations with the Bashaw, where none was necessary.
American guns had already done the job. In the resulting treaty,
the ransoms were paid for the prisoners after all. Barron went
back to the outworn blockade tactics and Preble returned home
aboard the *John Adams*. He felt deeply over his replacement,
but an incident that took place before he sailed helped brighten
the homeward passage, and fittingly it was on the quarterdeck
of the *Constitution*.

Young Stephen Decatur, brave in his new captain's uniform, snapped to attention, then stepped forward and presented
the Commodore with a scroll, signed by every surviving member
of the great company of men and boys he had trained; severely,
yet with a fatherly interest, as if they were his own sons — as
in fact of accomplishment they were. The inscription read:
"We, the undersigned officers of the squadron late under your
command, cannot, in justice, suffer you to depart without giving
you some small testimony of the very high esteem in which we
hold you as an officer and commander."

Preble found it difficult to speak, but the cheers made a reply unnecessary. They set a pattern for the long passage home, for the world at large as well as his "boys" was quite aware of what he had done. The Pope wrote President Jefferson that Edward Preble and his little squadron off Tripoli, "in forty days has done more for the cause of Christianity than the most powerful nations in ages."

Testimonial dinners at Malta, Gibraltar and New York were followed by a reception at the temporary White House, and Congress voted him a sword and a gold medal. Admiral Lord Nelson even remarked to his closest associates that the smart manner of handling the new American frigates, and the frigates themselves, formed the nucleus of trouble for the Royal Navy.

The tired and now desperately ill old man from Maine had taken the raw material in men and building plans, and in a comparatively short time created that nucleus. He had started with outworn models and experimented to make a navy. He had taken boys and turned them into men, who not only could sail and fight the ships, but build them. He had taught them all he had known and more; to make the best of what little was available — to make that little count. He had taught them innovation, just as he taught shipwrights by trial and error. Above all, he had given them the will, the watchword, the code that has been the United States Navy's ever since. "Having decided on battle," Commodore Preble said, "we'll fight!"

It was the men he trained, of course, who actually made the Navy of the future. They were all Preble and Preble was in them all. He had set a pattern to fight any place, anywhere, and to fight efficiently. President Jefferson wanted to make him Secretary of the Navy, and his boys wrote him that they would be pleased if he did accept the post. His health answered for him; the long-time ulcers had become cancer of the stomach. He gave up all social activities and spent long days in bed. During his well periods he traveled between Portland and Boston, overseeing construction of some of "Jefferson's gunboats."

In June of 1807, the incident of the *Leopard* and *Chesapeake* shocked Preble. When he received a letter from the Secretary a week later asking him to take command for war, he wrote in reply, "I am very low, but will obey if I am obliged to be carried on board. The occasion will soon restore me."

In August, the Portland man who was called the Father of the United States Navy, died. The legacy that he left his country in fighting spirit, integrity and devotion to detail that forms the Navy tradition is beyond reckoning.

And without doubt, it would please Edward Preble mightily to be remembered above all his many honors, as a Blue Water Man from the State of Maine.

THE BLUE WATER MEN have long since sailed their tall ships over the misty horizon into the pages of history. Men of ideas as well as action, with business acumen extraordinary, they played a major role in making the United States the great nation it is today.

To name them all would take several volumes, but the strength of character stemming from a Puritan ancestry is indicated by the portraits that have come down to us; the stiff facial lines, the severe set to the jaw, the unsmiling lips. There is distance in the cold eyes, a self-reliance, and the knowledge of a job well done.